Portraits of UNIQUE HOMES

A LUXURY PERSPECTIVE

VOLUME II

1993

Portraits of
UNIQUE HOMES

Written by Shelley Nohowel

Edited and compiled by Richard A. Goodwin
With assistance from Kathleen Carlin,
Lauren Hauptman, Kenneth Hunt,
Susan L. Pisut and Ilene Schechter

Senior Art Director Donald J. Tesoriero,
Art Direction and Design by Alan Dittrich
and Kristine Jones

Production by Carole A. Harley
and Angus Stopford

A UNIQUE HOMES PUBLICATION

Table of Contents

A PASTORAL PERSPECTIVE

Belvedere
Orange County, Virginia, Pages 44-49

Ross Valley Farms
Monkton, Maryland, Pages 50-55

The Ranch JMS
Near Willis, Texas, Pages 56-61

A WATERFRONT PERSPECTIVE

Indian Harbor
Greenwich, Connecticut, Pages 12-17

A Treasured Retreat on Gem Island
John's Island, Vero Beach, Florida
Pages 18-23

Contemporary Overture
Concord, Massachusetts, Pages 24-29

Artists in Residence
Incline Village, Nevada, Pages 30-35

Craig Knowe
Seal Harbor, Maine, Pages 36-41

A CELEBRITY'S PERSPECTIVE

Gloria Crest
Home to Gloria Swanson in the Late 1930s
Englewood, New Jersey, Pages 64-69

Vinton Valley Ranch
Between Malibu and Calabasas, California, Pages 70-75

The Bobby Vinton Estate
On Lido Key, Sarasota, Florida, Pages 76-81

Carol Burnett's Island Life
Honolulu, Hawaii, Pages 82-87

Sylvester Stallone's Place in the Sun
Miami, Florida, Pages 88-93

Beaver Dam Farms
The Country Retreat of Kenny and Marianne Rogers
Near Athens, Georgia, Pages 94-99

AN OLD WORLD PERSPECTIVE

Château Thal
In Belgium, Near the German Town of Aachen
Pages 102-107

A Screen Gem
Pasadena, California, Pages 108-113

Oak Knoll
Mill Neck, Long Island, New York, Pages 114-119

The Tower of Lethendy at Miekleour
Perthshire, Scotland, Pages 120-125

An English Manor Reborn
Lake Forest, Illinois, Pages 126-131

Floralyn
Lattingtown, Long Island, New York, Pages 132-137

A GRAND SCALE PERSPECTIVE

Purity in the Desert
Rancho Mirage, California, Pages 172-177

A Contemporary Classic
Old Westbury, Long Island, New York
Pages 178-183

Tous les Siécles
Rancho Santa Fe, California, Pages 184-189

Dean Gardens
Near Atlanta, Georgia, Pages 190-195

Camelback Villa
Paradise Valley, Arizona, Pages 196-201

A PANORAMIC PERSPECTIVE

1049 Fifth Avenue
New York City, Pages 140-145

Bellavista
Santa Ana, Costa Rica, Pages 146-151

Homage to the Modernists
Pomona, New York, Pages 152-157

Urban Aerie
Chicago, Illinois, Pages 158-163

Landmark on the Peninsula
Woodside, California, Pages 164-169

Preface

When it was determined that there would be a second volume of "Portraits of Unique Homes," I was a bit skeptical. I'd just been handed the 'can you top this?' task of finding even more spectacular properties to showcase than the year before, and in less time. In the course of my search I learned many things, among them: There will never be a shortage of exceptional residences for sale, and similarly, there are apparently no limits when it comes to the sense of pride and pleasure such homes convey to their owners. As you'll see in the pages ahead, "home" can mean different things to different people. For one family it's a 16th century castle that comes with its own barony title; for another, it's a state-of-the-art contemporary masterpiece atop a mountain with breathtaking views in every direction.

In assembling these pages, there have been interviews with artists, architects and even aristocrats. We've read the writing on their walls, found a few ghosts in the closets, and unearthed some wonderful hidden treasures. Every owner has a unique and sometimes humorous story to tell about the place he or she calls home. And, as you look into these living rooms and libraries, bedrooms and backyards, you'll quickly realize that each house tells an equally compelling story about its owner.

As editor, I am merely one of numerous individuals responsible for the creation of this book. I express my gratitude to the brokers and agents who have introduced Unique Homes to these extraordinary properties, the photographers who have captured the "good life" on every page, and my tireless editorial, art and production staffs. Lastly, my sincerest thanks to those people who have graciously allowed us to come into their homes and have shared their wonderful stories with us all. Without them, this book would not be possible.

Richard A. Goodwin

Buying a Lifestyle

Jensen-Willard is distinguished for its fine reputation, in-depth knowledge of real estate, dedicated service and award-winning advertising. The firm specializes in waterfront properties, historic homes, harbor views, country living and condominium convenience.

Jensen-Willard territory, based in Southport and Westport, begins at water's edge and extends into the rolling countryside of Fairfield County. The company's market includes condominiums from $80,000 to estates valued at $10,000,000 or more.

Expect the best when you pursue the Fairfield County Lifestyle—away from the hustle and bustle, into the heart of history—and only 50 miles from Manhattan.

Betty Jensen   Melanie Willard
Clarisse Loughran   Sarah Keenan   Pat Randolph
Chris Kehoe   Mary Helen Williams   Stephanie Inglis
Anne Lanzo   Bill Newman   Mary Ann Batsell   Pat Henstenburg
Diane Jones   Renée Janssen   Jack Jensen   Jill Kelly   Judy Rawlings
Barbara Downey   Pat Diefendorf   Cindy Thorburn
Linda Burnham   Phyllis Edwards   Dick DeJounge
Sallie Codman   Mimi Baldwin

ESTATES CLUB
THE ART OF MARKETING PROPERTY.

JENSEN-WILLARD
R E A L   E S T A T E

OPPOSITE SOUTHPORT POST OFFICE IN-THE-VILLAGE
411 PEQUOT AVENUE, SOUTHPORT, CONNECTICUT 06490

(203) 255-1001

RECOGNIZED BY
WHO'S WHO IN LUXURY REAL ESTATE

Your pool in the valley, lake in the mountains, marina at the shore, stream on the farm...

All just one phone call away.

"Home" means so many different things to different people. For some, it is a palatial estate high atop a mountain, for others a rustic beachhouse on the shore. A ranch in Montana, a condo in Hawaii.

No matter what your taste, your lifestyle, or your location, there is most likely a CENTURY 21® office close at hand. That's because our network consists of more than 5000 offices, staffed with tens of thousands of real estate professionals ready to serve your needs.

Best of all, you can access this vast network with just one local phone call — to the CENTURY 21 office nearest you or toll-free 1-800-221-7920.

So whether you're moving around the corner or around the world, whether your needs are simple or complex, whether your tastes are extravagant or modest, there is no real estate sales organization better equipped to help you find the home of your dreams than the CENTURY 21 system.

It's no wonder that — year in and year out — the Brokers and Sales Associates of the CENTURY 21 system help sell more homes than any other real estate sales organization on earth.

1-800-221-7920

A *Waterfront* PERSPECTIVE

ABOVE: *For nearly a century, the mansion built by Elias Cornelius Benedict has been a landmark for sailors and the gem of the Greenwich shore-line.* OPPOSITE: *Surrounded on three sides by water, Indian Harbor encompasses the promontory that once was home to Boss Tweed's infamous "Americus Club." Since it was built, the estate has been praised for its magnificent blend of nature and architecture.*

Indian Harbor

Greenwich, Connecticut

History remembers E.C. Benedict as the son of a poor Presbyterian minister who joined the New York Stock Exchange at age 29 and devoted the next 54 years to amassing a mighty fortune at the brokerage firm he founded. He sailed some half a million miles during his lifetime, from the choppy coast of Maine to the steamy heart of the Amazon. He was an old salt whose favorite drink, it has been told, was sea spray served up with a West Indian hurricane. But he remained every bit a gentleman of integrity and intellect—mentioned on two occasions as a candidate for governor of Connecticut (he declined the honor both times), commodore of the revered Seawanhaka Corinthian Yacht Club (following William Vanderbilt) and personal confidant to some of the highest-ranking political figures of his day. It was on the Oneida, Benedict's 200-foot steam yacht moored in Greenwich Harbor, that President Cleveland "quietly" underwent surgery for a malignancy in his jaw.

Long after his name is forgotten, what will remain is perhaps Benedict's greatest legacy: the home known as Indian Harbor. For a man much in love with the sea, the rocky promontory that had once been home to Boss Tweed's notorious "Americus Club" could not have been more perfect: 80 acres of potential grandeur with parklands to the north, Greenwich Harbor to the west and Long Island Sound to the south and east.

In 1895, Mr. Benedict engaged Carrére & Hastings, architects of the New York Public Library and the Frick Mansion, to replace the then-standing Indian Harbor Hotel with a landmark of his own: a three-story Italian Renaissance villa embraced by an assortment of cottages, a farm, an icehouse, carpenter's and

painter's shops, a gas house with floating dock, a coal house and a water tower with windmill. Carrére & Hastings not only built a formidable residence, but also fashioned wisteria-covered pergolas that step-terraced down from the west facade, an allée of maples ushering the way to the porte cochere, beds of perennials, working greenhouses, a complex of conservatories and a 150-foot terrace culminating at either end in broad steps leading to the bathing beach and a landing dock.

It is obvious Benedict derived great enjoyment from living the high life at Indian Harbor. The 30-room stucco villa was host to many a newsworthy event, but none perhaps more extravagant than the May 1900 marriage of his daughter, Helen, to architect Thomas Hastings. A special train brought more that half of the 800 guests from Grand Central Station to Greenwich, and a processional of some 145 carriages escorted hundreds from the Second Congregational Church to Indian Harbor for the reception. The Clevelands, the Carnegies, and architects Stanford White and Charles McKim were

OPPOSITE: *A large circular drive approaches the stately porte cochere along the mansion's front facade.* TOP: *The formal library centers around a carved stone fireplace. Wood-paneled walls and an elaborate coffered ceiling are also featured.* ABOVE: *A wall of windows in the solarium captures a dazzling panorama that includes Greenwich Harbor and the Long Island Sound.*

among the guests that afternoon.

Following E.C. Benedict's death in 1920, subsequent owners carried on a tradition of merry-making that had virtually become a requisite at Indian Harbor. The children of one owner recollect sailing off to the private island in order to ride the family's horses. They also swam in a salt-water pool which was created at the edge of the Sound. Others who grew up here remember with devilish delight the basement's labyrinthine complex of tunnels, private chambers and underground escape routes, presumably leftovers from the notorious days of Boss Tweed.

The estate no longer requires a staff of 40 to keep things running smoothly, as it did when Benedict was alive. The property now measures over 10 still-stunning acres (including the three-acre island offshore) with enchanting terraces and walkways, a large greenhouse, pillared gazebo, tennis court, mooring and the original clock tower standing guard at the entrance. The most recent owners, Edwin ("Jack") and Elizabeth ("Betsy") Whitehead, transformed a mansion that their children remember as "a bit too ostentatious" into a sanctuary of pure enjoyment—removing the heavy Italianate gilding,

glassing in the veranda for a spectacular year-round solarium, transforming the cavernous basement into an indoor resort complete with bowling alley and wine cellar, and bringing much love to the home.

Confides one of Mr. Whitehead's step-children, "I can still remember the time Bobby Short came to play. The living room was emptied out—everything except for the carpet—and then filled with cafe tables draped in shiny lamés. I also recall sitting up on the roof while my mother and Jack had these huge outdoor parties. At one of them, my step-father sank the motor boat and the rescue squad had to tow all these dripping, well-dressed ladies back to shore. But best of all were Saturday and Sunday mornings. At 10:30 a.m. Jack would head for the tennis court, and my mother would be close by, puttering away in her rose garden. Afterwards, they'd have lunch together, and then just the two of them would go off sailing. Their adoration for one another just seemed to fill the place with goodness."

Photography by Michael Forester.

Indian Harbor was presented in Unique Homes by Robert Wilder, Coldwell Banker/Previews® Schlott Realtors®, Greenwich, Connecticut.

🏛 ℭHARACTERISTICS

PROPERTY SIZE: Seven-plus acres onshore; three-acre island offshore.

ARCHITECTURAL STYLE: Mediterranean villa.

WHEN BUILT/RENOVATED: Built in the 1890s; renovated throughout the 20th century.

SQUARE FOOTAGE: Approximately 15,000.

NUMBER OF BEDROOMS: Six principal.

NUMBER OF BATHS: Nine principal.

OUTBUILDINGS: Nine-car garage in clock tower, also with upstairs apartments; greenhouse; gazebo.

DISTINCTIVE ARCHITECTURAL DETAILS: French doors, towering Palladian windows, distressed oak floors, semi-circular verandas, extensive wood paneling, coffered ceilings, eight fireplaces, century-old handcarving throughout.

SPECIAL APPOINTMENTS AND/OR AMENITIES: Lower-level bowling alley and wine cellar, waterside pool and courtyard, squash and tennis courts, deep-water dock and adjacent floating dock.

A Treasured Retreat on Gem Island

John's Island, Vero Beach, Florida

For a little over 20 years, John's Island has been evolving into the first prize of Florida's "Treasure Coast." To one side of this barrier island, there's the ocean with three miles of clean sand beach, a posh and rambling clubhouse complex, and grand-scale Georgian mansions housing elegant oceanfront apartments. To the western side, things get a bit sportier but no less deluxe. There are three 18-hole golf courses laid out by Pete Dye and Tom Fazió, tennis and squash courts, restaurant and pub-style dining, and private residences focusing on birdlife, fairways and the Indian River (also known as the Intracoastal Waterway). John's Island has no hotels or T-shirt shops. What it does have are about 1,700 acres of civilized lushness with water at every boundary.

The latest addition to this quiet enclave, an easy drive north of Palm Beach, is Gem Island, a 79-acre haven accessible to the John's Island property via a bridge crossing. It was here, just two years ago, that the first of 41 estates (all waterfront) was built by architect Jim Gibson, whose Regency designs have become something of a signature for John's Island. The look is smooth plaster walls, splashing fountains and shaded colonnades, very high ceilings and cool floors of stone and marble. There's nothing new wave.

OPPOSITE TOP: *The newest development in prestigious John's Island, Gem Island is a 79-acre enclave surrounded by the waters of the Indian River. It will be home to, at most, 41 residences.* LEFT: *Architect Jim Gibson designed this Regency-style home, ideal for the yacht owner with its deep-draft access on the Intracoastal Waterway.* ABOVE: *High ceilings, pickled oak parquet floors, a marble fireplace and French doors with fanlights create a traditional formality in the living room.*

🏛 CHARACTERISTICS

PROPERTY SIZE: One acre.

ARCHITECTURAL STYLE: Regency home on the water.

WHEN BUILT/RENOVATED: 1991.

SQUARE FOOTAGE: Approximately 5,000 under roof.

NUMBER OF BEDROOMS: Three (in main house).

NUMBER OF BATHS: Three and one-half (in main house).

OUTBUILDINGS: Two two-car garages, pool/guest house.

DISTINCTIVE ARCHITECTURAL DETAILS: Teak paneling and pickled oak cabinetry, custom-laid floors of marble, shellstone and pickled oak parquet. Classical columns used indoors and out, ceilings ranging from 12 to 16 feet, extensive fittings of marble.

SPECIAL APPOINTMENTS AND/OR AMENITIES: Large vaulted country kitchen which combines cooking, breakfast and family room areas. Elegant master suite with adjoining exercise/sitting room, marble bath salon, dressing area, walk-in closets and privacy garden. Guest accommodations in main house and in cabana. Pool, spa, veranda, brick patio, established plantings and 80-foot deep-water dock .

ADDITIONAL HIGHLIGHTS: This was the first home built on Gem Island, the newest addition to the John's Island Club. It has substantial Indian River frontage as well as a lake view, and it's being sold with a club membership. It is one of the few properties around with deep-draft access, making it ideal for a yacht owner. Gem Island is approximately 79 acres in size and will contain no more than 41 private estates.

This first Gem Island house has what the owners consider the best setting of all, as it is surrounded by age-old oaks, magnolias and palms, and strategically set between the river and one of several lakes on the island. It's a watery scene complete with a brick-terraced pool and an 80-foot dock providing deep-draft access. "Originally we had a home at the Ocean Reef Club in Key Largo. Then we moved to Boca, but it wasn't for us," says the owner, a retired ad agency executive who now divides his time between New Jersey and John's Island.

From his own yacht, he's seen all the clubs up and down the waterway, and he claims there's no place like this. Unique to this part of coastal Florida are the ancient live oaks, wildlife and an incomparable amount of green. A mile or so away there's a hard-packed dirt road known as Jungle Trail—still undeveloped along the river and canopied in moss-covered oaks.

"We don't spend very much time indoors," the owner

OPPOSITE TOP: *With a fireplace, wet bar and built-in shelves, the paneled library is a quiet personal retreat.* OPPOSITE BOTTOM: *A glimpse of the master bath salon, which includes a marble walk-in shower, an oversized tub overlooking a private walled garden, a dressing area, a sitting/exercise area and large his-and-her walk-in closets.* BELOW: *The beamed kitchen area combines cooking, dining and family room areas into one magnificent space.*

claims, though the interior is indeed equally enticing. His wife has done most of the decorating, with occasional collaboration by local decorator Frank Lincoln. Both husband and wife supervised the fitting of the teak wood paneling in the library, as well as floors of marble, pickled oak parquet and Mexican shellstone. Commenting today on the expert millwork, the stately columns inside and out, the 16-foot ceiling heights, the broad veranda and sweeping views, the owner claims with appropriate satisfaction, "Thomas Jefferson could have lived here."

The expensive, airy layout has about 5,000 square feet under roof, with plenty of privacy areas including the library with its wet bar and fireplace, the walled garden and the exercise area off the master suite, the two guest bedrooms and another living arrangement in the detached pool cabana with its own kitchen and bath facilities. But, one glimpse of the country kitchen reveals where the real living takes place. Here, beneath a vault-

ABOVE: *Classical columns separate the living room from the formal dining room. This open floor plan is conducive to entertaining and maximizes the natural light in this area of the home.* TOP RIGHT: *With one of Gem Island's lakes in front of the home and the Indian River (Intracoastal Waterway) to the rear, this estate offers a wealth of water views.* BOTTOM RIGHT: *The sun-drenched pool area is beautifully set between the residence and the frontage on the Indian River.*

ed ceiling beamed in cypress are a cooking island and wet bar, pickled oak cabinetry, a large bay window, breakfast area and family room alcove. It's one grand space where meal preparation, eating, drinking and entertaining happen easily.

The openness of the home is again well defined in the two more-formal rooms—the living and dining areas separated by towering white columns. Through French doors, this elegant space leads out to the pool terrace and spa, the pool house and the river beyond. Dockside, the owners watch the porpoises charting their own course up and down the river. In their private study hangs a memento from boating days gone by. The "Lady Julia" name plate was given to them by a friend when they owned a 38-foot Hatteras. The expanse of this plaque was a bit too large for the boat, maintains the owner, but in a room that resembles a captain's paneled stateroom, it has found a fitting place in their home.

Photography by Kim R. Sargent.

This Gem Island estate was presented in Unique Homes by the John's Island Real Estate Company, Vero Beach, Florida.

Contemporary Overture

Concord, Massachusetts

I n a town typifying staunch and steady New England, there's nothing nostalgic about the place. It's culture shock for anyone leaning toward clapboard cottages, log cabin quilts and Colonial colors. There is no "yesteryear" in sight, making it one of the great quirks of Concord—a town about as firmly entrenched in America's beginnings as one is likely to find.

In a sequential series of volumetric spaces where glass walls rise three stories high, the house displays enough cream-colored clapboard to side a small Early American village. But any traditional overtones abruptly stop here. Rooflines are defined by smooth tomato-red "barrels" built of tin. Various wings bisect one another in an asymmetrical layout spanning some 18,000 square feet. There are curving galleries, dramatic lofts and spatial twists at every turn. Monochromatic themes and a never-ending expanse of polished oak floors are interrupted at whim with bold strokes of color. And throughout the house, there is a continuous focus on the out-of-doors.

This contemporary tour-de-force is the centerpiece of more than 20 privately owned acres near the Concord/Lincoln town line, less than half an hour northwest of Boston. In building the house, great care was given to leave its natural surroundings intact, specifically the forest groves, wildflower meadows and wetlands

OPPOSITE TOP: *Warm, neutral clapboard, red tin arching roofs, and spontaneously placed windows, balconies and bays define the exterior of this exciting contemporary.* LEFT: *The asymmetrical, horizontal layout of the home has been designed to work with—rather than against—the quirkiness of the New England landscape.* ABOVE: *The indoor pool features a spa, a diving board and quadraphonic Bang & Olfsen underwater sound.*

🏛 CHARACTERISTICS

PROPERTY SIZE: $20^{1}/_{2}$ acres overlooking Fairhaven Bay on the Sudbury/Concord River, with views also of the Concord National Forest.

ARCHITECTURAL STYLE: Clapboard contemporary with curving rooflines and lofty three-story windows.

NUMBER OF ROOMS: 16.

SQUARE FOOTAGE: 18,000.

NUMBER OF BEDROOMS: Six.

OUTBUILDINGS: Detached three-car garage with two-bedroom caretaker's apartment.

DISTINCTIVE ARCHITECTURAL DETAILS: Huge glass window walls, strong geometric planes and angles, blond oak hardwood floors, gallery/loft levels, interior pilasters, indoor and outdoor balconies. The house is designed in a series of interconnected wings positioned for endless water and woodland views.

SPECIAL APPOINTMENTS AND/OR AMENITIES: Bold, organically-shaped Italian furnishings, textured-weave walls, custom lighting and climate control systems, state-of-the-art security, high-tech home entertainment center, private downstairs apartment, and separate library wing with office. One wing, referred to as the "pool house" features an indoor pool, Finnish dry sauna, bath and changing rooms.

ADDITIONAL HIGHLIGHTS: Championship tennis court, fitness trails and access to a nearby boat launch. Great care has been taken to preserve the natural beauty and privacy of this setting, and the existing landscaping incorporates forest groves, wildflower meadows, and river wetlands in their natural state.

along the Sudbury/Concord River. As it has for generations, the land abounds with wildlife and pastoral views. Together, these elements all have a softening effect on the angular geometry of the house. The synthesis is both surprising and complete.

Indoors, there is a refreshing sense of spontaneity in these well-ordered wings. Bold, organically shaped furnishings designed by Saporiti of Italy bring the dimensional impact down to earth. Cabinets of deep desert blue, chrome fixtures and galvanized steel lighting accessorize a kitchen that is both fun and functional. The children's wing is appropriately young in design, filled with primary colors and lofty 20-foot ceilings, while the library wing offers a more adult setting with its office,

OPPOSITE TOP: *A sitting area shares a see-through fireplace with the salon.* OPPOSITE BOTTOM: *The view from one end of the living wing looking toward the step-up salon, which occupies the opposite end.* BELOW: *The colorful eat-in kitchen includes striking cabinetry, chrome fixtures, galvanized steel lighting and a fully equipped cooking island.*

reading area and fireplace.

Scale, light and form bring an inescapable feeling of energy to the house that serves as a compound for work, entertaining and private family living. Leisure time here may be spent on fitness trails, on the championship tennis court or in an indoor pool equipped with underwater quadraphonic sound. There are Swedish massage jets in the master bath and a Finnish dry sauna adjoining the pool. The courtyard brings together natural and man-made elements in three descending pools linked by rocky waterfalls and a contemporary white footbridge.

In a daring and decisive approach to living, new age has come to New England with a great sense of architectural freedom.

This contemporary estate was presented in Unique Homes by Sotheby's International Realty, Boston, Massachusetts, and Brigitte Senkler & Associates, Concord, Massachusetts.

ABOVE: *One end of the library wing features a well-appointed office, while the other houses a quiet reading area with fireplace.* TOP RIGHT: *The courtyard is a magical outdoor space adorned with flowering Oriental trees and shrubs as well as three descending natural pools linked by waterfalls. The focus here is a contemporary footbridge.* BOTTOM RIGHT: *The neutral color scheme maximizes the impact of the contemporary art found throughout the home.*

Artists in Residence

Incline Village, Nevada

I t's nearing Memorial Day on Lake Tahoe. Against the northern rocky reaches, towering pines are reduced to miniature playthings by the unceasing heights of the Sierras, still laced with snow where their peaks touch the clouds. Down at water's edge, it's already another season. There are flowering plums and creeping phlox in bloom. Boats are being readied for their buoyant return to the lake. The summer sun is making its annual, dappling debut on fountains, ponds and waterfalls. It's an alpine scene lacking only the distant sound of cow bells. Though, from the grand Renaissance château, this too seems possible.

Of the home she started building about a decade ago, Sharon Croom says, "It was an experience that is mine forever." And she says this with such passion that you know from the start the experience was a good one. Sure there were those tough times ("carrying a work crew through three of the worst winters in memory in order not to lose them...building section by section under heated tents"), but in her years as job supervisor and

ABOVE: *The estate's three and one-half acres are set against the majestic backdrop of Lake Tahoe and the mountains beyond.*
RIGHT: *The work of scores of highly skilled artisans went into the creation of this handsome residence. Though it was built less than 15 years ago, the mansion—with its towering chimneys, turret and window bays—evokes all the romance of an old world château.*

chief designer, she came to many important realizations. Among the more fundamental was: "This isn't about banging up boards and living in a box."

It was an "if you build it, they will come" scenario. Some 55 local craftspersons and artists found their way to the château during its evolution; and like the generations of masons and carvers constructing a cathedral, each one made his or her indelible mark. A loving wife and caring mother who had done "all the traditional things," Sharon Croom saw three and one-half acres on Lake Tahoe as the start of something big. "I had to prove something to myself," she says. Her husband George, she recalls, really wasn't keen on the idea, but finally did acquiesce with a simple "If this is what you really want."

If, upon completion, their princely palace wasn't already a showplace on the shores, it made itself so the day the Crooms hosted their first big party—an outdoor Renaissance fair for 700 or so guests, all of whom arrived in period costume. "I think they were well into the party before they even got here," says Sharon when describing some of the antique outfits. Refreshments consisted primarily of finger food ("they didn't use forks or knives back then," she adds) and libations from a climate-con-

trolled wine cellar on the premises. Along walkways that weave through the manicured grounds, many of the artists who had worked on the château set up booths to display their handiwork. "It was an opportunity to make others aware of these wonderful talents," she explains.

Sharon Croom also has a prevailing concern for giving something back to the community—cultivating and cleaning up county lands that reach just beyond their property, restoring the original stream that is now filled with trout traveling toward their natural spawning ground, and "getting dirty" for five hours a day in the gardens of the château.

"The house is an integral part of the grounds," she says. This is perhaps best illustrated in the kitchen. In a space for cooking, dining and relaxation, the room combines the view of a captain's bridge with the voluptuousness of a Tiffany mansion, its wedding-cake ceiling inset with stained glass panels inspired by the Wisteria Window the Crooms had seen at the DeYoung Museum. Directly above on the second floor of the turret, a similar water view unfolds from the master bath. The leaded and stained glass, plaster ornamentation, arching windows and alabaster-like finishes are all of museum quality.

OPPOSITE: *Inspired by Tiffany's Wisteria Window, the ceiling in the kitchen is a fantasy in glass equalled only by the view of azure waters and snow-capped peaks seen through the room's many windows.* ABOVE: *The gracious blend of warmth and style in the formal dining room makes this space well suited to entertaining.*

ABOVE: *In the master bath, a circular tub affords an exquisite vantage point for taking in the panoramic waterfront.* RIGHT: *The living room features elegant appointments, generous dimensions and double doors to the rear grounds and gardens.*

🏛 𝒞HARACTERISTICS

PROPERTY SIZE: Three and one-half waterfront acres on the North Shore of Lake Tahoe.

ARCHITECTURAL STYLE: Grand European château.

WHEN BUILT/RENOVATED: Built 1980-83.

NUMBER OF ROOMS: 10.

SQUARE FOOTAGE: Approximately 8,000.

NUMBER OF BEDROOMS: Six.

OUTBUILDINGS: Guest cottage with attached garage.

DISTINCTIVE ARCHITECTURAL DETAILS: Turreted master bath and kitchen overlooking the lake, both with stained glass ceilings; leaded windows throughout; woodwork custom-milled on site, plasterwork molded on site.

SPECIAL APPOINTMENTS AND/OR AMENITIES: Mahogany paneled office, climatized wine cellar, elevator, elaborate security and communications systems.

ADDITIONAL HIGHLIGHTS: Sweeping lake and mountain views from waterfront lawns and gardens, ponds, cascading waterfalls and rocky trout stream. Pier with two boat lifts. Immediate access to world-class resort activities year-round.

Save for their own furnishings and a host of high-tech treats (an in-house elevator, a television that mysteriously drops down from the ceiling in the master suite, an elaborate communications system and a garage that magically converts to an elegant banquet hall), virtually every fitting for the château was milled, molded or cast on site. During construction, their wood shop created a mahogany bar for the recreation room, elegant paneling for the owner's office, even a number of beds for the six bedrooms within the home. Seeing it all come together, says Sharon, "was a psychic satisfaction." Her only regret—"that I didn't have more confidence in myself"—is nowhere in evidence.

When asked what detail in the house, whether minute or majestic, is most indicative of her, Sharon responds after some thought: "The gardens. This is where it all becomes a whole." This is where she found her being and gave it so much beauty.

Photography by Mark Sinclair.

This majestic Lake Tahoe château was presented in Unique Homes by Bob Wheeler, Wheeler Associates, Inc., Incline Village, Nevada.

Craig Knowe

Seal Harbor, Maine

Its name is Scottish for "Rocky Knoll," which tends to be very appropriate for this craggy southeastern coast of Mt. Desert Island. But its setting suggests something lovelier still and far more lush. Amid gardens owner Molly Taggart has greened for over 20 years, her house is a stepping stone between earth and heaven. Looking at properties with her husband in the early 1970s, she kept returning to the cottage they'd seen with its well-established New England simplicity, its vistas to the sea and what she calls "its great vibes." The Mississippi native who now lives most of the year in New Orleans makes the transition from sultry to salty every summer—getting the Seal Harbor itch around mid-June and savoring her Maine life well into September.

Molly Taggart is a grandmother of four, an active member of the Garden Club of Mt. Desert, an avid hiker and mountain climber, and very much a seaworthy lady. "When the family gathers up here around the time of my birthday in August, I charter Dick Savage's boat and we go off and anchor at a nearby island for a lobster picnic. Afterwards, some hike, some swim, some nap in the sun." Back in New Orleans, a bit of spunky Maine is still in her heart when she serves her Southern guests Indian pudding and a traditional New England seafood casserole.

What she brings from New Orleans to Maine is sun drenched cheer and a passion for flowers. "I just have a small city garden filled with roses down here," she says with a note of apology. At Craig Knowe, the house is virtually embedded in blooms. Baskets of begonias number in the dozens on the 75-foot-long porch that overlooks the ocean and the

Gracing the crest of "The Hill" in exclusive, yet understated Seal Harbor on Mt. Desert Island, Craig Knowe is a wonderful summertime retreat offering a wealth of colorful gardens as well as views of the Atlantic Ocean and the Cranberry Isles.

ABOVE: *One of the home's six fireplaces adorns the large and airy living room.* OPPOSITE TOP: *In keeping with the tradition of summer cottages on the Maine coast, the interiors at Craig Knowe have been furnished simply and comfortably. Shown here is one of the home's five family/guest bedrooms. Four staff bedrooms are also included in the layout.* OPPOSITE BOTTOM: *A charming sun room opens out to a garden setting.*

Cranberry Isles. Tubs of geraniums and lobelia are closer to ground, while window boxes along the wonderfully weathered cedar shingle facade are replenished each summer with frothy mounds of impatiens.

Born in Picayune, Mississippi, Mrs. Taggart has a good dose of earth's bounty in her blood—her father and grandfather both having worked in the lumber business. Beneath pines that reach toward the sky and an idyllic horizon of blue gather gardens of Bonica roses, veronica, potentilla, clematis, delphinium, astilbe, hydrangea and rhododendron. You can't look out a window without a view that is awash in color.

Inside what the Maine vernacular modestly calls a "Bar Harbor cottage," Molly Taggart has covered over the original dark woodwork and "those ugly red brick fireplaces" with a soft palette of pastels. There is an abundance of white wicker and sheer drapery (or nothing at all) on the French doors and windows, a scattering of antique carpets on hardwood floors the color of maple syrup, and a few treasured items atop the mantels of six original fireplaces. With virtually every room having access to the first- and second-floor porches, the lightness is inescapable. She's not made that many changes to the home's turn-of-the-century design. There's still the old telephone room on the staircase (a secret hiding place that's irresistible to grandchildren). Up until the year Mrs. Taggart's grown children gave her a phone for the kitchen, this little closet was communications central for the entire household!

What Molly Taggart calls her "sweet, simple house" is a rambling old thing of beauty built in 1901 by New York architect J. Howard Chamberlain. There are five bedrooms and nearly as many staff rooms, sun and breakfast rooms, an authentic country kitchen with two pantries,

living and dining rooms, partial attic and basement levels along with a separate garage. It's 5,000 square feet in size with well over an acre of privacy and limitless views all around. It's steps from Acadia National Park, where Mrs. Taggart enjoys her walks with nature, and just up the hill from the finest sailing waters in New England. It's within earshot of the bobby clank of buoys and the sounds of the last lobster boat coming to shore at dusk, yet is never intruded upon by the noise of civilization.

"Every year when I fly into the Bangor Airport, my little Datsun station wagon is there waiting for me. I make the hour-plus drive home and go out to see the gardens," says the owner, speaking from her home in New Orleans. She seems as perennial about the place as are her plantings. This is truly a home of many happy returns.

Photography by Storey Litchfield.

Craig Knowe was presented in Unique Homes by LandVest, Portland, Maine.

🏛
𝒞HARACTERISTICS

PROPERTY SIZE: 1.2 acres with ocean and island views.

ARCHITECTURAL STYLE: "Bar Harbor" cedar-shingled cottage.

WHEN BUILT/RENOVATED: Built in 1901; renovated.

NUMBER OF ROOMS: 13.

SQUARE FOOTAGE: 5,000±.

NUMBER OF BEDROOMS: Five (plus four-bedroom staff wing).

NUMBER OF BATHS: Three and one-half.

OUTBUILDINGS: Detached two-car garage.

DISTINCTIVE ARCHITECTURAL DETAILS: Broad 75-foot-long rear covered porch overlooking the ocean, French windows and doors throughout, elegant picture moldings, 38-foot balcony on second floor, well-preserved hardwood floors.

SPECIAL APPOINTMENTS AND/OR AMENITIES: Six fireplaces (including one in master suite and one in foyer), playroom on basement level, two pantries situated off country kitchen, old world "telephone room" on the landing of the stately main staircase.

ADDITIONAL HIGHLIGHTS: Magnificent and well-established perennial gardens, superb views, private woodlands—all in one of New England's most sought-after coastal settings. Located on Mt. Desert Island, minutes from exclusive Bar Harbor, Acadia National Park and a host of sailing, tennis and swim clubs. Public golf courses also nearby. Ocean is two blocks away.

OPPOSITE: *On more than an acre complete with woods, lawns, gardens and water views, this classic shingle "cottage" was built in 1901 by architect J. Howard Chamberlain and features approximately 5,000 square feet of interior space.* ABOVE: *Running most of the length of the home is a large covered porch, perfect for relaxing and casual entertaining against a backdrop of stunning water views.*

A Pastoral PERSPECTIVE

Belvedere

Twenty minutes down the road from Thomas Jefferson's Monticello, and immediately adjacent to James Madison's Montpelier, the Greek Revival manor known as Belvedere is about as firmly entrenched in historic Virginia as any home built within the 20th century. Constructed around 1908 by William DuPont, the 177-acre estate was originally known as Gaston Hall; and after a succession of subsequent owners, some locals started referring to the place as "Ghastly Gaston Hall." The house and its grounds required great attention and enormous fortitude from its next occupants if it was to last into the next century. Fortunately, some loving admirers arrived, bringing with them the right mix of vim and vision, and a palpable passion for history.

They came down from their home in Canada during the centennial of the Civil War and immediately saw "serenity." They also saw lawns cluttered with dead oaks and poison ivy, wood barns not suitable for Thoroughbreds, and clay walls so thick that the installation of a modern air conditioning system became a year-long endeavor. "We were only going to do this once and we insisted it be done right," says the lady of Belvedere who, after nearly 20 years in residence, has clearly acquired a perfect balance of compassion, conviction and Southern grace.

And she certainly hasn't minded getting her hands dirty in the process. All the

ABOVE AND LEFT: *Both Georgian and Greek Revival influences can be seen in the architecture of the three-story manor that is at the heart of the estate known as Belvedere. Built in 1908 by William DuPont, the home has been meticulously renovated without diminishing in any way its architectural integrity.*
RIGHT: *Belvedere is also a superb farming property which includes state-of-the-art mare and yearling barns, oak plank fencing in its nine paddocks, a farm manager's house and much more. In all, the property encompasses some 177 acres.*

45

exquisite green gardens are her handiwork. Beginning with the herb garden and continuing through boxwood parterres, brickwork and crimson-colored beds of salvia, one can't help but believe her when she says she hasn't had a fingernail in 15 years. Each of the gardens has been designed in memory of a loved one who has passed on. "It was the best way I knew to deal with my grief."

The formality of these gardens is mirrored in the refined presence of the Georgian home, where Jeffersonian design prevails on many levels. In traditional center hall fashion, the front porch, where Doric columns support a pediment with Palladian-style window, proceeds into a 37-foot-deep foyer. It, in turn, opens out again onto the back veranda overlooking the gardens, swimming pool and a jewel box of a gazebo. Flanking the main hall are living and drawing rooms (one front, one back), a dining room filled with lemon-colored Chinese wall coverings and a modern kitchen.

Both side elevations of the three-story residence

ABOVE: *Housed in its own wing is the two-tier library, complete with walk-around gallery, bookshelves, glassed-in display cabinets and Adam-style fireplace.*
LEFT: *Also in a separate wing, the ballroom features a 20-foot-high beamed ceiling with decorative inserts and a minstrel's gallery.*
RIGHT: *A handsome marble mantelpiece and built-in shelves grace the living room.*

🏛 CHARACTERISTICS

PROPERTY SIZE: 177± acres.

ARCHITECTURAL STYLE: Greek Revival and Georgian.

WHEN BUILT/RENOVATED: Built by William DuPont circa 1908. Renovated and restored over eight years in the late 1970s and early 1980s.

NUMBER OF ROOMS: 16.

NUMBER OF BEDROOMS: Five bedrooms, plus in-house staff apartment.

NUMBER OF BATHS: Seven.

OUTBUILDINGS: State-of-the-art mare and yearling barns, isolation barn, storage barn, run-in sheds, two original structures not renovated (wood barn and old brick carriage house), plus a four-bedroom farm manager's residence.

DISTINCTIVE ARCHITECTURAL DETAILS: Doric columns on front and back porches, 12- and 20-foot ceilings, hand-painted Chinese wall coverings, original interior pine shutters flanking Jefferson windows, antique marble fireplaces, beautifully milled overdoors, double-height ballroom and library.

SPECIAL APPOINTMENTS AND/OR AMENITIES: All new wiring, nine-zone heating and cooling, swimming pool, gazebo and extensive formal green gardens.

ADDITIONAL HIGHLIGHTS: Near Thomas Jefferson's Monticello and immediately adjacent to James Madison's Montpelier.

extend into two-story wings: to the left, a majestic library with walk-around gallery open to the floor below, and to the right, the ballroom—a thing of beauty with its beamed 20-foot ceiling, minstrel's gallery and large Gothic-style fireplace. Yes, the owners have had a ball or two here, along with charity events, evening concerts and the like.

The particulars of each room reveal still more history. The carved Italian marble fireplaces found in the living and drawing rooms appear remarkably similar to those at the nearby Madison home. The staircases also bear a striking resemblance to the ones in Montpelier. The magnificent interior shutters, now stripped down to their original pine finish, frame floor-to-ceiling Jefferson windows that open the dining room and drawing room to the front porch. Also in the drawing room are deeply set overdoors embellished with antique Wedgewood plaques that the current residents brought back from England.

Following in the footsteps of Thomas Jefferson, who brought a wealth of European influence in domestic design to this country two centuries ago, the owners have

ABOVE: *Highlights of the formal dining room include a yellow siena marble fireplace dating back to the late 19th century, two shell corner cabinets and hand-painted Chinese panel wallpaper.* OPPOSITE TOP: *Extending the full width of the house is the gracious entrance foyer with fireplace.* OPPOSITE BOTTOM: *Of the five bedrooms in the main house, three are master-sized, including the "Rose Room" pictured here.*

filled their home with exquisite 18th century furnishings, imported carpets and fabrics, and a substantial collection of antique paintings. Today they maintain Belvedere is a "bit overstuffed...but that's okay, we're collectors."

The house lends itself to formal living, yet be mindful of one caveat: This is a blessedly unassuming part of the country, and if there's no mud on your boots, people are going to know you're from out of town. It would appear the travel writer who recently called these parts "the Santa Fe of the East Coast" may have been a bit off the mark, consciousness-wise. "It's a pretty big secret how wonderful this place is," say the owners, who scarcely need to remind us they've been doing their part to keep it that way.

In what they call their "grand manor at home with nature," the owners of Belvedere share an obvious affinity for animals, enjoying most of all the afterglow of sunsets, when rabbits and deer come out to graze, with

the lingering hues of the Blue Ridge Mountains not so far away. Their love for horses is also very much in evidence. The two state-of-the-art mare and yearling barns, run-in sheds and various other farm dependencies have been built with serious equine interests in mind. To complement the main house, there is a farm manager's residence which they totally rebuilt during the estate's eight-year-long renovation.

This Virginia couple maintains a residence in Manhattan, but the truth is, it's hard to leave the home they've named Belvedere (Italian for a building designed to look out upon a pleasing scene). Flying in or out of the Charlottesville Airport, they grab a window seat, look for the red salvia in bloom and know that they've found home. According to the transplanted Canadian, wife, mother, resident historian and gardener of Belvedere, "When I say to my farm manager or friends that I'm off to New York for a week, they take bets on when I'll really be back. It's usually only two or three days."

Photography by Philip Beaurline.

Belvedere was presented in Unique Homes by Stevens & Company, Charlottesville, Virginia.

TOP LEFT: *The formal living room, featuring an antique English mantel, affords gracious surroundings for displaying fine furniture and art.* BOTTOM LEFT: *An antique chandelier and exquisite wallpaper embellish the formal dining room, which adjoins the glass-walled solarium.* ABOVE: *Ross Valley Farms, encompassing 237 acres in the heart of Maryland's horse country, is one of the finest facilities of its kind in the United States.*

Ross Valley Farms

Monkton, Maryland

Seventy years ago, if you were horsey enough to hunt with the Vosses and the Ladews, or race with the Vanderbilts and the Whitneys, chances are you'd have found yourself on Long Island amid a well-heeled coterie of families striving to keep their equestrian interests intact. In the name of "progress," developers who could scarcely distinguish between a polo field and a dressage arena began stripping the north country of its happy hunting grounds, and a great migration southward ensued.

Half an hour north of Baltimore, the grass was greener, the winter kinder, and the social climate agreeably more relaxed. Here one could really get down to the business of horses. Before long, Edward Voss became lifetime master of the Elkridge-Harford hounds, Alfred Vanderbilt was settled at Sagamore Farm (a 21st birthday present from his parents) and there were more miles of white board fence than public or private roads combined.

It was this right mix of the rural and the refined that prompted a native of Louisville to purchase an 18th century farm in Monkton in the early 1980s. Her story is a familiar one—starting out with one Thoroughbred riding

horse and an assortment of aged farm buildings that remained from an original dairy operation. Less than a decade later, the 237-acre breeding facility known as Ross Valley Farms had evolved into one of the area's most pristine equestrian settings (the kind of place where they admit to vacuuming the driveway on occasion). The historic dependencies were thoroughly restored, eight miles of board fencing were white-washed to a fare-thee-well, and the owners built a new main residence, pool house and farm manager's home on these grounds once traversed by the Grand National Hunt.

All the right visuals are here: classic 200-year-old barns, verdant pastures and spring-fed ponds, rolling hills, grazing Thoroughbreds, stone-walled gardens and four full-time attendants to keep things running smoothly. No less attention has been paid to the home itself, a Mid-Atlantic farmhouse with a wonderful mix of important antiques, warm woods, and flower-filled fabrics. The two-story great room with its fieldstone fireplace and the latticed solarium bring formal and informal spaces together; while walls of glass, wraparound verandas, blue-stone patios and the architecturally compatible pool-house broaden the home in every direction.

To the uninitiated, there is one huge, hovering

🏛
𝒞HARACTERISTICS

PROPERTY SIZE: 237 acres.

ARCHITECTURAL STYLE: Traditional manor.

WHEN BUILT/RENOVATED: Mid-1980s.

NUMBER OF BEDROOMS: Three full suites.

NUMBER OF BATHS: Four full, two half-baths.

OUTBUILDINGS: Totally and authentically restored 18th century stone barns (two) and guest house, new tenant house and pool house.

DISTINCTIVE ARCHITECTURAL DETAILS: Imported mantels, pegged oak floors, pine paneling, lavish fabric treatments, Palladian windows and cathedral ceilings.

SPECIAL APPOINTMENTS AND/OR AMENITIES: Massive stone fireplace in two-story great room, state-of-the-art kitchen, marble baths, lower-level office and exercise room, central vacuum and custom lighting systems.

ADDITIONAL HIGHLIGHTS: A professional Thoroughbred breeding operation combined with an exceptional residential compound, including illuminated gardens, wrap-around porches and patios, and swimming pool.

dilemma. How do you spend a day on the farm, help out a mare in foal, get down to the business of selling yearlings, keep up with five grown kids (three currently in the horse business) and still manage to greet dinner guests in a house filled with antique carpets, gleaming oak-pegged floors, heirloom mantelpieces, marble baths and antique sconces? "No problem," maintains the owner. "You just make certain you have a mudroom!"

Satisfying every horse and human whim looks effortless here, which means the farm ranks right up there with the best of them. You simply go from breakfast to box stall to bathing suit to black-tie, and take comfort in knowing that your neighbors are probably doing just the same. And if you're lucky, you might have the time to get up to Saratoga in August.

Photography by Richard Lippenholz.

Ross Valley Farms was presented in Unique Homes by Marilyn Hoffman of Hoffman Realty International, Dallas, Texas.

OPPOSITE: *Included in the facilities at Ross Valley Farms are two totally and authentically restored 18th century stone barns, a restored stone house ideal for guests, and miles of white board fencing.*
ABOVE: *The 40-foot pool with hot tub is great for summertime relaxation, while the pool house—equipped with wet bar and full bath—facilitates casual entertaining.*

The Ranch JMS

Near Willis, Texas

A hundred years ago this was premium tobacco country. Earlier still it was settled by pioneers who negotiated land rights from Old Mexico. The last cotton gin to operate in Montgomery County stood on Old Houston-Danville Road, which leads into the property now known as The Ranch JMS. The name comes from Joe and Marion Scates, who came to east Texas from the Gulf Coast in 1981 and saw a rare opportunity for calm country living 52 miles from Houston. "The lay of the land was wonderful," recalls Marion, "a bit overgrown and requiring much imagination, but still wonderful." Today, she maintains there's not an inch on the 300-acre ranch that she doesn't know well. "Over there are oak trees the deer sleep under in the wintertime." Another tree she points to is a live oak planted around the time of the Civil War.

The centerpiece of this vast tract, where the Texas coastal plains meet up with the Timberlands region, is the Scates residence, a contemporary variation on a French Country theme with pastoral views in every direction. Most of the 11,000-square-foot interior happens on the main level, and virtually every inch is

ABOVE: *A rustic wood sign announces the entrance to the ranch.* RIGHT: *Complete with an abundance of exquisite cabinetry and commercial appliances, the professionally designed kitchen is open to a large entertainment area. The traffic flow through the kitchen, informal dining area, sun porch, billiard room, and kitchen sitting area was designed to accommodate informal gatherings on a Texas-size scale.*

detailed in oak that was custom-milled on site. "I wanted the warmth of wood without an overly masculine look," explains Marion, and she avoided heavy overtones at every turn with leaded glass, French doors and floor-to-ceiling windows. There was no way this house could darken. The addition of shaded breezeways and loggias throughout further emphasized its openness.

The 14-room interior is filled with favorite things such as Western bronzes by Tom Moss, contemporary glass sculpture by Mexican artist Patricia Baez, and an assortment of fine Sarouk and Kashan carpets. The heart of the home is Mrs. Scates' kitchen without walls. "I decided if I was going to have to cook, everyone would have to join in," she says with a Southern smile. Dining, entertainment and bar areas are all a part of this wonderful space, as is the long open porch which suggests further opportunities for casual entertaining and Texas-style barbecues.

The exterior design of the home, all old Chicago bricks with a well-worn look, is echoed indoors with

OPPOSITE: *A handsome marble fireplace with classic mantel and an antique Sarouk rug establish an elegant, formal tone in the living room.* TOP: *The main residence is a country French-style home of grand proportions.* ABOVE: *For entertaining, the formal dining room is situated directly across the entry hall from the living room.*

BELOW: *French doors from the billiard room and kitchen area open to the large covered porch.*
OPPOSITE TOP: *The first-floor master suite includes a large bedroom and a private bath which adjoins a sun room featuring hot tub and exercise equipment.*
OPPOSITE BOTTOM: *Encompassing approximately 300 acres, the ranch features ideal terrain for the raising of Thoroughbreds.*

brick fireplaces in the billiard room and sitting area. A marble fireplace graces the living room, a more formal space with period-style pieces and European lighting. Like the kitchen, the master suite is yet another wonderful indulgence. It has its own glass-filled solarium where one can watch the world go by from the swirling waters of a hot tub. The more energetic will also appreciate that this space is equipped with first-rate exercise equipment.

At one time the Scates maintained as many as 35 brood mares on the ranch and were actively breeding and raising halter colts. Today the JMS operation has been scaled back a bit, with just a few pleasure horses and some cattle. The property remains, however, a premium site for a serious ranch operation. There are no less than 40 stalls in the various barns and sheds, plus a covered arena, breeding barn with laboratory, 14 paddocks, 10 fenced pastures, hay and machinery barns and six ponds. All have been created within the past decade or

so, as have the guest house, office building and three additional residences which are privately set away from the main house as well as from each other.

What keeps Marion Scates active these days seems to range from attending the ballet in Houston to fly-fishing in the wilds of Colorado and Wyoming (a pastime she calls her "Zen"). She's also on the Board of Trustees of the Greater Houston Women's Foundation. Her greatest love, though, seems to be spending time at home with a good-size flock of children and grandchildren, surveying the scene as hawks, owls and deer feed in the meadow behind the house. Amid the hearty native Texas trees, towering pines and oaks, hers is a very peaceable kingdom.

Photography by Machel Elam and George Gomes.

The Ranch JMS was presented in Unique Homes by Beth Wolff, Beth Wolff & Associates, Inc., Houston, Texas.

🏛 Characteristics

PROPERTY SIZE: 301 acres.

ARCHITECTURAL STYLE: Country French.

WHEN BUILT/RENOVATED: Built 1981-83.

NUMBER OF ROOMS: 14.

SQUARE FOOTAGE: Principal—7,300; under roof—11,000.

NUMBER OF BEDROOMS: Four (in main house).

NUMBER OF BATHS: Four full, two half-baths.

OUTBUILDINGS: Guest house and office building plus three smaller homes. Two horse barns, breeding barn, foaling shed, 12 horse sheds (each with two paddocks), feeding sheds, hay and machinery barns.

DISTINCTIVE ARCHITECTURAL DETAILS: Old Chicago bricks used for exterior of house as well as two of the three fireplaces. Leaded glass entry doors, top-quality oak millwork throughout, 10-foot ceilings on main level, plantation fans in nearly every room.

SPECIAL APPOINTMENTS AND/OR AMENITIES: European-style lighting, catering-capacity appliances in kitchen, spa and workout room adjacent to master suite, main-level guest suite, billiard room, darkroom, four-zone air conditioning plus fire and security systems.

ADDITIONAL HIGHLIGHTS: Low-maintenance grounds of towering pines and oaks, 90 acres of fenced hay pasture, 120 acres of commercial pine and hardwoods, plus several fenced pastures and ponds.

A Celebrity's PERSPECTIVE

Gloria Crest

Englewood, New Jersey

The Mediterranean mansion on North Woodland Street was a local legend long before Gloria Swanson bought the place in the late 1930s and enrolled her daughter in a revered private school nearby. It was Count Stefan Poniatowski, one-time heir to the Polish throne, who built the glazed tile and brick residence in 1926, creating his own palace just across the Hudson River from Manhattan. With medieval turrets and limestone walls, a king's ransom in gold leaf and silk brocade, vaulted ceilings and imported tapestries, the 20-odd rooms of the house appear straight out of an 18th century château. One has to wonder how it has survived the modern world, as all the previous owners have taken their furnishings and antique treasures with them.

"My husband and I have one favorite hobby: collecting," says the current owner of Gloria Crest. "We've mixed Italian, French and English pieces from all the periods. We follow our hearts, buy what we love, and it all seems to work." She is a native of Holland who has long considered New Jersey her home. He is a commercial real estate developer whose parents came from

ABOVE: *The grand reception foyer makes a dramatic statement with its sweeping dual staircase, ornate bronze railings, classic chandelier suspended from a domed limestone ceiling, and 24 karat gold leaf trim.*
RIGHT: *Reminiscent of a lavish villa on the Mediterranean, Gloria Crest was built in 1926 and encompasses some 12,000 square feet of living space.*

Poland. They purchased Gloria Crest in 1976 when given first option by a good friend, the son of the previous owner. Today, they recall, there was never a moment's hesitation. "It was love at first sight."

Entering the home, it's rather easy to envision Ms. Swanson in a commanding descent on the grand double staircase, readying for her close-up with Mr. De Mille. "I've never seen 'Sunset Boulevard'," admits the owner, "but many friends have assured us this could be the very staircase." At the top, where the steps from both sides are joined in a formal balcony, the owners have hung a 19th century Russian tapestry depicting a wedding scene. Standing guard at each end are suits of Italian armor, and overhead is one of the many massive chandeliers that seem perfectly scaled for the grandeur of Gloria Crest.

Directly ahead of the staircase is the formal dining room, detailed with a host of leaded windows, a carved stone fireplace, and cognac-colored English oak paneling. The marble floors in this room, as well as those in the foyer, are of creamy travertine. "My husband made

OPPOSITE: *The music room is an elegant entertaining area which adjoins both the living and dining rooms.*
TOP: *A massive carved stone fireplace is a focal point in the living room.*
ABOVE: *Leaded windows, marble flooring, an ornate fireplace and English oak paneling establish a formal tone in the dining room.*

ABOVE: *A Chinese motif embellishes the turret room, accessed by a spiral staircase leading up from the guest suite.* OPPOSITE TOP: *The guest bedroom itself is a handsomely appointed chamber. A sitting room, dressing room and bath are also part of the suite.* OPPOSITE BOTTOM: *The approximately five acres of grounds include formal gardens, a lily pond with fountain, goldfish pond and natural lake.*

the decision to re-floor these two areas with something more in keeping with the original limestone walls; something that looked like it belonged." Beyond are the gilded living room with arched entrances to a solarium with goldfish pool, a mahogany library banked by bookcases and French doors, and a music room properly attired for tea concerts or after-dinner chamber music.

A consummate hostess and guardian of old world traditions, the lady of the house maintains, "There are few places where black-tie really belongs today. This is one of those houses. Our parties tend to be very elegant, very formal—it's what the house was meant for." This reverence for the way things were extends to the lavish Jacobean guest suite, the walnut-paneled bar where draft beer is tapped from the cool basement, and to the grounds themselves—five acres of stately gardens, ponds and terraces that seem to be in constant denial of the fact that Manhattan is only minutes away. Yew trees which had grown to darken the grounds have been clipped and sculpted into regimental stands of topiary, and crowded evergreen masses have been thinned to bring an abundance of light to Gloria Crest.

Perhaps the only real indication of concessions made to the 20th century are the two new kitchens in this 12,000-square-foot house: one filled with Sub-Zero and Thermador appliances on the main level, the other downstairs convenient to the staff suite and wine cellar. When asked, both husband and wife admit that cooking is of no interest to them, but they do enjoy entertaining greatly. Any caterer would be quite content here.

There is no favorite room in the house. Both owners have spent the better part of their 25-year marriage making every space a visual feast, from the formal breakfast room with its three exposures of arching windows overlooking the gardens, to the "turret room," reached via spiral staircase leading from the guest suite. Here, the owners leave Europe and journey east amid the Oriental carpets and cachepots, a central Pagoda-shaped lantern and lacquered trim painted in the traditional Chinese red and black. They invite four or five friends in for dinner, she puts on her Geisha robe, and it's carry-out from a nearby Chinese restaurant.

It's not always black-tie at Gloria Crest.

Photography by Gil Amiaga.

Gloria Crest was presented in Unique Homes by Murphy Realty, Tenafly, New Jersey.

ᴄHARACTERISTICS

PROPERTY SIZE: Approximately five acres.

ARCHITECTURAL STYLE: Mediterranean villa.

WHEN BUILT/RENOVATED: Built in 1926.

NUMBER OF ROOMS: 20.

SQUARE FOOTAGE: 12,000.

NUMBER OF BEDROOMS: Four (plus two for staff).

NUMBER OF BATHS: Three full, two half-baths (plus two for staff).

DISTINCTIVE ARCHITECTURAL DETAILS: Marble floors, limestone walls, carved stone fireplaces, extensive paneling (mahogany, oak and walnut), plus original finishes of gold leaf, silk brocade and bronze.

SPECIAL APPOINTMENTS AND/OR AMENITIES: Museum-quality public rooms, solarium with goldfish pool, paneled bar room, "turret" rooms reached by private staircases above the master and guest suites.

ADDITIONAL HIGHLIGHTS: A former residence of Gloria Swanson, situated on re-established park-like grounds within minutes of New York City.

Vinton Valley Ranch

In California, between Malibu and Calabasas

The indoor pool area at Bobby Vinton's California ranch is a truly magnificent space, as ideal for recreation as it is for casual living and entertaining. Also functioning as an enormous solarium, this space has retractable panels in the ceiling and walls, a private bathroom, flagstone flooring and an array of tropical trees and plants.

BELOW: *A decidedly rustic flair characterizes the design of the generously sized living room. Outstanding appointments in this room include a soaring cathedral ceiling with clerestory to accentuate the natural lighting, massive wood beams and supports, lustrous hardwood flooring, a grand flagstone fireplace and French doors.* RIGHT: *Encompassing approximately 100 acres, the ranch includes a stocked lake, a natural creek and a host of mature plantings.* BOTTOM RIGHT: *The fireplace in the living room was built from stones found on the property.*

Bobby Vinton admits he has a tendency to act a bit impulsively when it comes to buying real estate. He made the decision to purchase his waterfront home in Sarasota, Florida, after being in town just one day, and after just one drive-by. His one-time home in Hollywood (which he and his wife later sold to Steven Spielberg) he bought without ever having stepped inside. In the case of the 100-acre California ranch acquired in 1989, it was nothing less than a primal urge. "I grew up in a little mill and mining town not far from Pittsburgh," Vinton explains. "My father bought the place for $2,400. When a car drove by, my bedroom shook. When I wanted to play ball, I did so in the street."

At Vinton Valley Ranch, Bobby Vinton has found the quiet, privacy and room to roam he never had as a child. "Sometimes I think life happens backwards. We should be born old and just get younger every year. That way, after all the hard work, we'd be young enough to enjoy things!" The man has a unique philosophy to life, and an insatiable urge to keep moving. Most recently the family home was in Malibu, where the traffic was in front, the beach out back and neighbors literally on top of them. "You couldn't whisper without someone in the next house hearing you," says Vinton. "We finally got away from all that." Escape they did, to the heart of the Santa Monica Mountains between Calabasas and Malibu. It's 35 minutes away from Beverly Hills and a country mile

ABOVE: *The stone and wood main house was situated on the property to take advantage of natural breezes. Once it was built, Vinton went to the expense of having 100-year-old oak trees moved closer to the residence.* OPPOSITE TOP: *Hand-painted tiles add a colorful accent to the beautifully designed gourmet kitchen, which is equipped to handle all entertaining needs.* OPPOSITE BOTTOM: *Pictured here is one of the four guest/staff cabins.*

from anything. There are Thoroughbred horses and log cabins built of fragrant cedar trucked in from Wisconsin. There's a private lake stocked with bass and a natural creek meandering about. There are fruit orchards, rose gardens and year-round produce from a hothouse that caters to the Vinton's nearly vegetarian way of life.

Speaking from one of the guest cabins he has transformed into an office, Bobby Vinton sounds a bit more like a Ponderosa rancher than a legendary recording artist. "A hundred years ago this land was all outlaw country, and there's still only one road that leads into the place." He adds, "We built the fireplace in the living room from stone found right here, and probably spent $200,000 moving 100-year-old trees closer to the main house once it was built."

The house he refers to is a huge, happy homestead of natural stone, warm wood and glass, where 25-foot ceilings, oak floors and staircases, and hand-painted cabinetry fit well within the theme of casual grandeur. The indoor swimming pool also functions as a lofty solarium filled with greenery and surrounded by retractable glass walls and ceiling panels. With flower-filled fabrics and carpets, the house is alive with color.

Approximately one-fourth of the Vinton's 12,000-

square-foot residence is reserved for the master suite. Here the owners relax beside an English marble fireplace in the sitting room. Nearby are a hidden wet bar and equally well-concealed projection TV. Separate wardrobe rooms link up with a master bath designed with heated marble floors, a steam shower and spa tub.

"I always wanted a place where the family could all be together...a compound of sorts. And when we do, these are the happiest times. These are my best memories," reflects Vinton. Wearing the riding pants in the family are his three daughters, who enjoy the ranch's first-class equestrian setting with riding and training rings, several pastures, a six-stall barn and miles of scenic trails. Mrs. Vinton gets into the gardens, while the man of the house is putting in his own driving range.

Amid flowers, mountaintops, sea breezes and sunsets over the nearby Pacific, it's busy leisure at its best. It's vintage Vinton.

Photography by Paul Jonasen.

The Vinton Ranch was presented in Unique Homes by Kay Cole and Sarah Campbell, Rodeo Realty, a division of The Prudential California Realty, Woodland Hills, California.

🏛 ℭHARACTERISTICS

PROPERTY SIZE: 100± park-like acres.

ARCHITECTURAL STYLE: Wood and stone country house.

WHEN BUILT/RENOVATED: 1989.

SQUARE FOOTAGE: Approximately 12,000.

NUMBER OF BEDROOMS: Three.

NUMBER OF BATHS: Four and one-half.

OUTBUILDINGS: Four separate guest/staff cabins, hothouse, barn with interior and exterior horse stalls.

SPECIAL APPOINTMENTS AND/OR AMENITIES: 3,000-square-foot master suite with English marble fireplace, concealed wet bar and projection television; plus master bath with heated marble floors, steam shower, spa tub and wardrobe rooms. Indoor pool with retractable walls and ceiling. Screening room.

ADDITIONAL HIGHLIGHTS: Private lake stocked with bass, mature trees and exotic foliage, winding natural creek, first-class equestrian facilities with several pastures and miles of groomed trails, north/south tennis court with viewing area.

The Bobby Vinton Estate

On Lido Key, Sarasota, Florida

A few years ago when Bobby Vinton's performance schedule called for a night in Sarasota, the singer made time for an extra day of just looking around. And he was smitten with the place—the weather, the water, everything. He called up his old friend Perry Como, who was settled on Florida's east coast in the Jupiter area, and it was Como who suggested that Vinton drive over for the day and let some real estate brokers take him around. Bobby Vinton says he never made it past Lido Key, because once he had seen the Gulf-front house built in the 1950s by architect Philip Hess, he knew it had to be his. "The house was in no way like us," says Vinton of his wife and himself, "and that was the immediate attraction. It reflected a side of our personalities we never knew we had."

The home is a steel-reinforced Bauhaus-style box of concrete and glass, crowned by a circular solarium-projection room originally built for one of the previous owners, a French count who was also a film producer. Mr. Vinton says this room is a wonderful escape with its 360-degree views taking in Sarasota Bay and the Gulf of Mexico, along

OPPOSITE: *Handsome carved entry doors open to the grounds of Bobby Vinton's Sarasota estate, with views of the bay immediately seen through the glass walls of the main house.* ABOVE: *Built in 1956 by well-known architect and builder Philip Hess on Sarasota's New Pass, the striking residence has become a much-admired landmark on Lido Key.*

CHARACTERISTICS

PROPERTY SIZE: Two acres on Lido Key.

ARCHITECTURAL STYLE: Steel frame and glass contemporary overlooking approximately 300 feet of deep-water bay frontage.

WHEN BUILT/RENOVATED: Built in 1956; continually expanded and upgraded.

SQUARE FOOTAGE: Approximately 9,000.

NUMBER OF BEDROOMS: Five in main house.

NUMBER OF BATHS: Six and one-half.

OUTBUILDINGS: Two guest houses, gazebo, tennis pavilion (open-air).

DISTINCTIVE ARCHITECTURAL DETAILS: Carved entry doors, floor-to-ceiling windows, custom lighting, Mexican tiles on pool terrace.

SPECIAL APPOINTMENTS AND/OR AMENITIES: 360-degree roof-top solarium with elevator access, fully equipped dockage, 800-bottle wine cellar, walk-in vault, poolside wet bar, and outstanding sunset views over the bay.

ADDITIONAL HIGHLIGHTS: Prime waterfront setting on New Pass with views to the south end of Longboat Key and the Gulf of Mexico. Upon completion by well-known architect Philip Hess, the home was featured in *House Beautiful*.

with a profusion of plantings the count brought in from around the world. "We have trees with metal plates indicating the origin of each specimen, and they came from all over the place...Cuba, Borneo, you name it!" One of the previous owners, an industrialist with vineyards in France, reconfigured the house to make all the guest rooms the same size; this in an effort to make certain visitors would be equally pleased with their accommodations. He also added a wine cellar with an 800-bottle capacity plus a four-bedroom guest house overlooking the water. Yet another owner added deep-water dockage and the north/south tennis court.

The Vintons, whose preference is to spend more time outside than in, now have a home that is the quintessential destination for low-key luxury. An open-air tennis

OPPOSITE TOP: *Soaring window walls throughout the home open interior spaces to the panoramic water views.* OPPOSITE BOTTOM: *Ready to accommodate stylish parties, the dining room even comes with recessed ceiling lights positioned so that each place setting can be spotlighted.* ABOVE: *An abundance of Mexican tile surrounds the lavish pool, where a semi-circular wet bar, privacy walls and handsome plantings create an inviting setting for outdoor living and entertaining.*

pavilion edged in latticework and potted palms provides breezy respite from a workout on the court. Beside the pool, a semicircular bar is tucked among the Mexican tiles and handsome plantings. At dockside, there is ample room for resident craft and visiting yachts alike. Throughout the home, walls of floor-to-ceiling glass make this an environment of fresh air and sunshine. The owner admits even when he's in the shower (singing, of course), the windows are wide open and "I really belt it out!"

In case it's not already understood, Bobby Vinton, whose greatest hits include "Blue Velvet" and "Blue on Blue," happens to have a favorite color. Here the water and sky satisfy his thirst for blue. When asked what song has been kindest to him, Vinton says without hesitation,

" 'Blue Velvet'. Just last year the song was used in a television ad for Nivea skin lotion in England, and before long it was #1 on the charts there. The song just came to life all over again.

"I've always looked for new dimensions in my life," says the veteran performer with 10 gold albums, a 100-acre spread in the foothills of Malibu, a wife and five children, and a zealousness to living that seems several paces ahead of the rest of the world.

The next stop for the Vintons is Branson, Missouri, where they've found yet another side of their subconscious. This middle America town that's filled with lakes and plenty of peace and quiet has evolved into one of the country's most vital entertainment communities.

Like a proud papa, Vinton boasts, "It's got about 30 theaters and more seats (55,000) than on Broadway, and soon it will be home to my Blue Velvet Theater, complete with the Glen Miller Orchestra."

Best of all, Vinton adds, "I'm building a home there, and I can stay at home until five minutes before the curtain goes up. I can eat breakfast and lunch at home. And I can get to bed at a decent hour." It's a rare treat for someone who has spent more nights on the road and in hotels in Atlantic City and Las Vegas than he probably cares to remember.

Photography by Jack Elka.
Interior design by Joyce Hart of Robb & Stucky.

The Bobby Vinton Estate was presented in Unique Homes by Lynn Robbins, The Prudential Florida Realty, Sarasota, Florida.

Carol Burnett's Island Life

Honolulu, Hawaii

While the studios and stages of Hollywood and New York have been her thirst, Hawaii has been her therapy. For 25 years, Carol Burnett has entrenched herself in the serene island way of life; first in a home in Kapalua, Maui, and most recently on the shores of Diamond Head. She acquired this Oahu Contemporary in 1987, totally refurbished the place with her favorite things, and definitely made the house a home. In a living room filled with palms and Asian fabrics, there are photos of her three daughters along with longtime friend and Diamond Head buddy Jim Nabors. While she has a comfortable office in the home, Burnett admits most of her time is spent on the lanai in an oversized wicker chair overlooking an ocean view she calls her "postcard."

The setting is truly picture perfect in this stunning glass house with an overwhelming sense of native calm. Floors are covered in marble, white oak, imported tiles and Berber carpets. Pitched ceilings rise up to clerestory windows. The furnishings are simple, big and designed for deep-seated comfort. The colors are of the sea, sand and sunset—pri-

OPPOSITE: *From the covered lanai, a breathtaking ocean vista unfolds, beautifully framed by tall, swaying palm trees. Carol Burnett refers to this view as her "postcard."* ABOVE: *The rear of the house opens to a magnificent pool area, a perfect spot for entertaining friends just steps from the beach.*

CHARACTERISTICS

PROPERTY SIZE: 7,770 square feet with ocean and Diamond Head views.

ARCHITECTURAL STYLE: Island Contemporary.

WHEN BUILT/RENOVATED: Built in 1981; completely refurbished in 1987.

SQUARE FOOTAGE: 4,146.

NUMBER OF BEDROOMS: Five.

NUMBER OF BATHS: Five.

DISTINCTIVE ARCHITECTURAL DETAILS: Marble and white oak floors, covered lanai with open ocean views, pitched cathedral ceilings, clerestory windows, interior shutters, walls of glass. Home designed by Ossipoff.

SPECIAL APPOINTMENTS AND/OR AMENITIES: Designer pool, air conditioning and alarm systems, telephone switchboard, complete furnishings, separate guest quarters, one bedroom converted to owner's office, Asian-style fabrics and accessories.

ADDITIONAL HIGHLIGHTS: The Honolulu home of actress Carol Burnett, completely renovated and furnished by the owner. Located in a private gated community on the shores of Diamond Head with dramatic ocean and mountain views.

LEFT: *The attractive kitchen offers a very functional work area surrounded by views of the home's lush, tropical surroundings.* BELOW: *The dining room creates an intimate setting for entertaining.*

marily muted green, peach and tan. And the view is one of the island's finest: a beautiful pool, a canopy of palms, the sandy shores of Diamond Head and a very blue ocean beyond. Her home, designed by Ossipoff, is appropriately private, secure behind the gates of a private community in Honolulu.

The home is filled with some very personal mementos: a photo of Ms. Burnett and Tom Selleck, with whom she performed "Love Letters" at the Diamond Head Theatre; and a framed letter from Lon Chaney dated June 4, 1923, given to the actress from a head writer and producers of the "The Carol Burnett Show." In obvious abundance are Carol Burnett's frogs—frog baskets, frog candle holders, wooden frogs from Thailand, jade frogs, ceramic

ABOVE: *One of the home's bedrooms was converted by Ms. Burnett into an office and the adjoining sitting room shown here.* LEFT: *The master suite opens to a lanai and spectacular ocean view.*

frogs, you-name-it-frogs. People started giving her frogs after her off-Broadway debut in "Once Upon A Mattress" (the story of Princess Winifred, who came from the bogs and the frog ponds...the other side of the tracks). "They've been good luck for me," says the Texas-born star, whose early days in the less-than-best section of Hollywood have certain parallels to the story of the princess who only wanted to live "happily ever after."

Her time in Hawaii has been private and deservedly indulgent, yet anything but hermetic. Burnett has generously instituted scholarship programs at the University of Hawaii and Diamond Head Theatre. "In Hawaii, espe-

cially," she says, "a few television shows have to hire a lot of technical people from the Mainland. It would be wonderful to train young people from Hawaii to take these jobs." During "down time" she frequents Kahala Mall and goes to the movies, something she never has time for in California; or she's out on the lanai reading scripts and catching up on the latest best-sellers.

Actually, it's hard to envision the "queen of TV revue comedy" having any time out at all. Since her 11-year, 22-Emmy-winning run with the "Carol Burnett Show," she has founded her own production company, Kalola (Hawaiian for "Carol"), launched "Carol & Company,"

produced her first movie ("Made in America") in tandem with Michael Douglas, and hosted the 25th anniversary of the show that made her a household name. Today, she's thinking about a home in Santa Fe, adding, "I'm not giving up the islands entirely."

She recently co-starred with Charlton Heston in "Love Letters" at the New Mexico Repertory Theatre in Santa Fe, and was instantly drawn to the spirit of the place. Ms. Burnett said in an interview with the Los Angeles Times, "It has a quality I liken to the Aloha spirit—the same feeling of peacefulness. It's a small town, but in a good sense."

In Hawaii, at her townhouse in Century City, at the home of a friend in Santa Fe, or in a hotel room in New York, she's one of those rare individuals who brings Aloha with her wherever she goes.

Photography by Ed Espero.

Carol Burnett's Diamond Head home was presented in Unique Homes by Patrick O'Neill, Coldwell Banker McCormack Real Estate, Honolulu, Hawaii.

Situated in sylvan seclusion next to historic Vizcaya, this estate is a wonderland of natural beauty. The canals were originally carved through the idyllic hardwood hammock in the 1920s by James Deering. Peeking out from behind the lush greenery is the main residence, a stately mansion combining contemporary styling with old world charm.

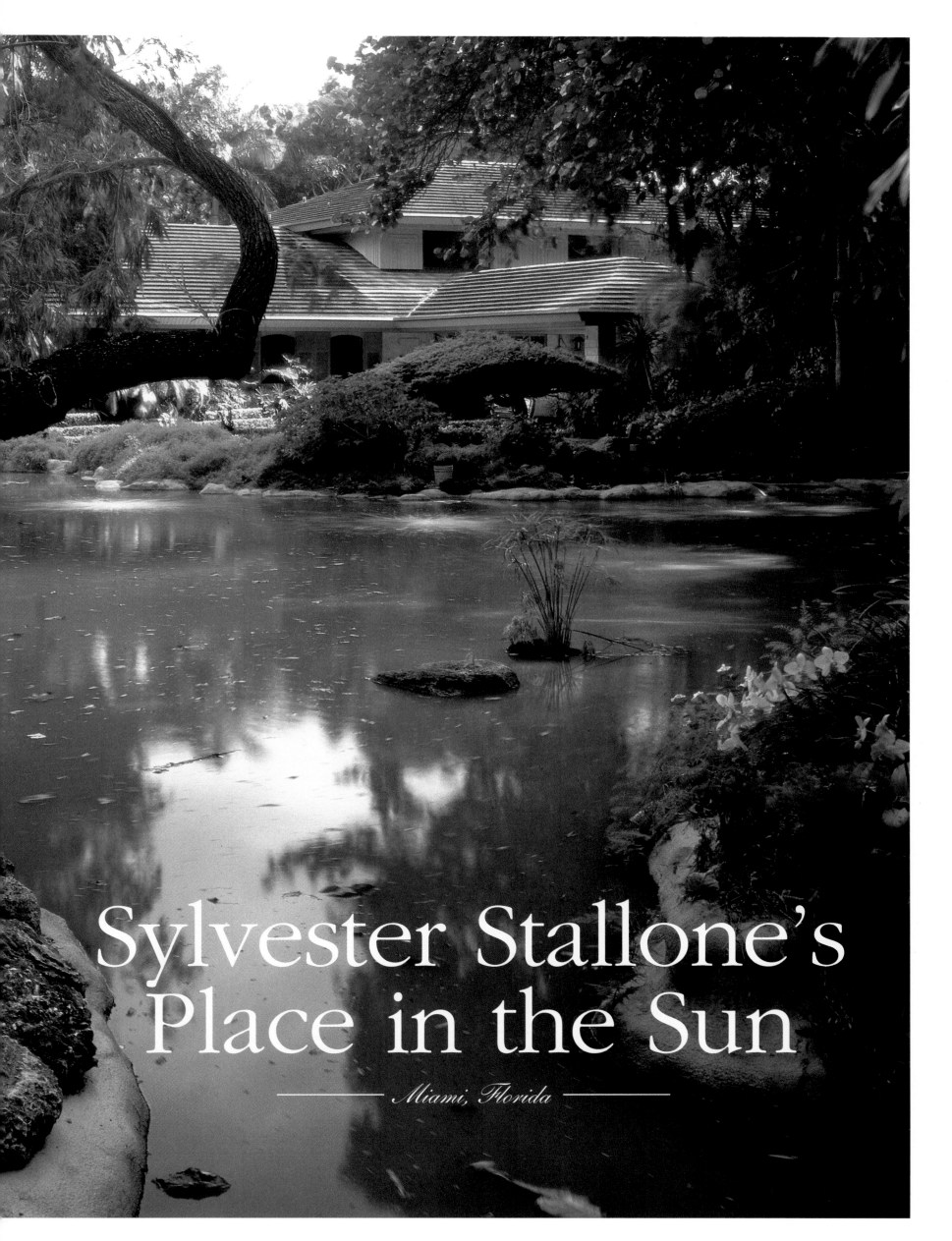

Sylvester Stallone's Place in the Sun

Miami, Florida

RIGHT AND BELOW: *A waterfall, meandering streams, a fern canyon and natural grottos set this incredible park-like estate apart from all others in the Miami area.* OPPOSITE TOP: *Large expanses of manicured lawn meet the 608 feet of seawall that runs along the estate's bay frontage.* OPPOSITE BOTTOM: *Flower beds add a colorful touch throughout the grounds.*

More than 1,300 miles of sun-drenched coastline surround the balmy peninsula known as Florida, the object of a land frenzy since the late 15th century, when Columbus claimed it sight unseen for Spain. It was not until the late 1800s, though, that some serious money started heading south and Florida entered an age of opulence. Hamilton Disston came down from Philadelphia and began a four million-acre real estate empire in the Orlando area. Thomas Edison moved from New Jersey to Fort Myers and built the first swimming pool in America. Retired Standard Oil baron Henry Flagler built a hotel, and a railroad straight to it. George Merrick created the country's first fully planned city. John Ringling brought the circus to town.

Another founding father, Chicago Industrialist John Deering, came to Miami with his own grand designs for wintering well—a 70-room villa in the fashion of the Italian Renaissance, complete with artwork and furnishings dating back to the 15th century. The setting was no less elaborate: a natural hammock overlooking Biscayne Bay with acre upon acre of formal gardens and splashing

fountains. Today, this is known to the public as Vizcaya Museum and Gardens. Right next door is the newly acquired home of Sylvester Stallone, situated on 11$^1/_2$ acres that were carved from the original Vizcaya property more than 35 years ago.

At the time Stallone purchased the property, it was Dade County's highest-priced residential estate, but it's not the kind of place you might expect of the roughed-up "Rocky" character or the survivalist in "Cliffhanger." And it's no Hollywood set. It is majestic oaks showered with orchids, leafy views to the blue waters of the bay, lighted fountains, meandering streams, a fern canyon and natural grottos. It is a private park of never-ending enchantment, sheltered behind an imposing main gate and still open to the sun and the sea.

It has been said Stallone wanted privacy as well as a world-class investment. What he also acquired was a home which would be impossible to duplicate in Beverly Hills. There is seawalled bay frontage extending more than 600 feet, with a dock large enough for a 100-foot yacht. Nearby, a charming boat captain's house overlooks a fish-filled canal. A gatekeeper's house is set

ABOVE: *Entrance to the estate is through an impressive main gate, just inside of which sits a roomy two-story, three-bedroom gatekeeper's house.* OPPOSITE TOP: *Paved and lighted pathways lead through lawn and hammock, from the main house to the guest house, dock, boat captain's house, gatehouse and various other outbuildings.* OPPOSITE BOTTOM: *The elegant estate residence is shaded by towering trees from the surrounding native hardwood hammock.*

immediately inside Vizcaya's original entry gates. A private orchid house measures some 12,500 square feet, while a shade house offers similar dimensions. And then there is the main residence, which was built in 1975 and spans another 28,000 square feet under roof.

The house is a brilliant blend of contemporary engineering and old world elegance, complete with a ballroom featuring a bronze minstrel's gallery and double-height arching windows overlooking the flower-filled grounds. The workmanship throughout seems from an earlier age. Five various woods are patterned on the floor of the sitting room. The library walls, window seats and bookcases are of Bermuda cedar custom-milled in the estate's own workshop. Folding mahogany doors link the family and formal dining rooms. A bath in the guest suite is fitted in star sapphire marble. The three-story staircase in the entry is a curving blend of marble and mahogany. Resting on solid rock that's 20 feet above high tide, the lower level of the house includes an enormous billiard room, wine cellar and an authentic tavern room brought

in its entirety from a 15th century Swiss château.

For all its magnificence, the home is at its best outdoors, in the cool shade of native hardwoods, on emerald colored lawns, amid banks of impatiens and azaleas, and overlooking Biscayne Bay. Paved and lighted pathways lead through the grass, gardens and hammock, linking the main house with the guest house and various other buildings. Along the way are delightful spots for lingering: a waterfall, a small bridge, a pond filled with koi and a meditation walk. In keeping with John Deering's vision of the perfect garden, there remain many of his original illuminated fountains. No doubt he'd be pleased to see the place looking so well.

Photography by Patricia Fisher.

This Miami landmark was presented in Unique Homes by Jeanne Nicastri, The Prudential Florida Realty, Coral Gables, Florida. Mr. Stallone's agent in the purchase was Evelyn Framer, Framer Realty, Miami Beach, Florida.

ℂHARACTERISTICS

PROPERTY SIZE: 11¹/₂ acres on Biscayne Bay, well protected in a hardwood hammock.

ARCHITECTURAL STYLE: Contemporary.

WHEN BUILT/RENOVATED: Built in 1975.

NUMBER OF ROOMS: 16.

SQUARE FOOTAGE: 28,000.

OUTBUILDINGS: Two-suite guest house, boat captain's house on canal, gatekeeper's house, enormous orchid house, shade house, equipment shed, carport and estate manager's office.

DISTINCTIVE ARCHITECTURAL DETAILS: Old world opulence throughout. Sweeping three-story staircase with solid mahogany handrail, two-story arched windows framed in bronze in the ballroom, bronze minstrel's gallery, marble floors, carved mahogany doors, library walls and bookcases of select Bermuda cedar.

ADDITIONAL HIGHLIGHTS: This sylvan property was carved from the original James Deering tract that now includes the Vizcaya Museum. The extraordinary grounds include meandering streams, majestic oaks, prolific orchids and more than 600 feet of seawall frontage on Biscayne Bay. Extending into the water is a reinforced concrete dock suitable for a 100-foot yacht.

Beaver Dam Farms

Near Athens, Georgia

When you're performing 200 concerts a year, hosting benefits for charity and building a nationwide restaurant chain, feeling your roots can be a bit of a challenge. It can also become a priority in life, as was the case for Kenny Rogers a decade or so ago. In 1981, he purchased a substantial 365-acre tract parceled off from a turn-of-the-century farm in Colbert, Georgia—a true mud-in-your-eye working farm that was totally self-sustaining with crops, livestock and the like. The site Kenny and Marianne Rogers bought had one lake on it; they added another seven or eight. They also cleared the way for their own main residence and guest house, clay tennis courts, a golf course and what has come to be known as one of the finest Arabian horse operations in the country.

It was some 10 years in the making, with much of the work overseen by Larry Hancock, the general contractor for Beaver Dam Farms who has since become executive vice president of Kenny Rogers Productions. The greatest challenge for Hancock came the day Kenny and he stood on a hillside and the conversation turned to barns; specifically, a 72,000-square-foot barn which would house 60 custom-built stalls, an indoor therapy pool and veterinary clinic, tack and wash rooms, executive offices, three apartments and a brass-railed show arena of somewhat dizzying dimensions.

ABOVE: *The gated main entrance to Beaver Dam Farms.* TOP RIGHT: *Designed by architect Henry Norris, the main house of over 20,000 square feet blends a number of architectural styles into an infinitely liveable and distinguished home.* BOTTOM RIGHT: *The living/dining area alone encompasses some 1,600 square feet and includes a carved limestone mantel and French doors opening to views of the private golf course.*

OPPOSITE: *A multitude of windows and a skylight drench the morning room with sun. The wooden spiral staircase shown here ascends to a private library and loft.* LEFT: *The master bedroom, measuring a spacious 24 by 40 feet, includes floor-to-ceiling French windows with European shutters and a custom-designed fireplace. Two master baths—one with a Jacuzzi, the other with a steam shower—and three walk-in closet rooms are also part of the master suite.* BELOW: *The five-bedroom guest house includes the gracious dining room seen here.*

"I visited all the major stables in Lexington, Kentucky, before embarking on this project," says Hancock, who had never built a barn of more than 12 stalls. "And then I came back here with a list of 105 mistakes to avoid." This structure and the very beautiful quarantine barn open out onto exercise and show rings, six fenced paddocks and seemingly endless pasture land.

For Kenny Rogers and family, home is a modern, breezy contemporary filled with warmth, sunshine and many personally designed details. The master suite is a 3,000-square-foot expanse that includes two baths and three walk-in closet rooms. In the bedroom itself, walls of French windows are fitted with European shutters that open and close at the touch of a switch. Elsewhere in the house, there are exquisite carved limestone fireplaces, marble floors, elaborate moldings, fabric-covered walls and custom furnishings. The mix is somewhat eclectic, but it all works well against earthy tones and natural fibers. A black granite table in the dining room is accompanied by lacquered Queen Anne chairs from Portugal. A Chinese alter table provides a handsome base for a impressive collection of Lalique. In the morning room, there are Luigi game tables; in the nursery, a four-poster log bed. From the morning room, where a floating spiral staircase leads up to the library and loft, French doors open onto a vine-covered pergola beside the swimming pool. Here in the Georgia sun, we see all that's irresistible about Beaver Dam Farms.

The tri-level pool terrace with its 5,000 square feet of patio surface leads to two championship tennis courts and verdant pastures beyond. Gentle lakeside plantings are canopied by towering live oaks, while the gardens are filled with azaleas, junipers and rhododendrons. This scenic interplay of color and texture continues onto the

🏛 CHARACTERISTICS

PROPERTY SIZE: 365-acre equestrian and golf estate.
ARCHITECTURAL STYLE: Contemporary.
WHEN BUILT/RENOVATED: 1981.
NUMBER OF ROOMS: 20.
NUMBER OF BEDROOMS: 11.
NUMBER OF BATHS: 13.
OUTBUILDINGS: Main barn (73,000 square feet) with three private apartments, 60 stalls, seven wash rooms, two feed rooms and tack room, plus observation and breeding rooms, on-site laboratory and equine pool. Gazebo-style lake house, five-bedroom guest house.
DISTINCTIVE ARCHITECTURAL DETAILS: Soaring windows and skylights, vine-covered pergola connecting house to pool, 25-foot ceilings, Italian marble floors, extensive moldings.
SPECIAL APPOINTMENTS AND/OR AMENITIES: 3,000-square-foot master suite, two kitchens, state-of-the-art intercom and security, carved limestone fireplaces, custom fabrics and finishes throughout.
ADDITIONAL HIGHLIGHTS: Lakes, waterfalls, terraces, horse barns, miles of bridle trails, award-winning landscaping, many custom furnishings and fittings, tri-level pool, two championship clay tennis courts and par-72, 6,145-yard golf course.

fairways and greens of Kenny Rogers' own golf course—a 6,145-yard, par-72 affair where all the hazards are indeed visual delights: pools, waterfalls, rock gardens, wooden bridges, pebble cart pathways and, of course, plenty of beaver dams.

The home has been a gracious gathering place for family members and close friends. It has also been site of the J.C. Penny/Kenny Rogers Classic, a star-studded "Olympics" hosted by Rogers to raise money for the homeless in Georgia. He's a good sport who's equally at ease in the saddle, playing tennis or basketball, or out on the golf course. "I can't really say the same for his fishing," laughs Larry Hancock, who claims the lakes here are filled with bass, carp and catfish.

In creating some rather remarkable roots for himself and his family, Kenny Rogers has also created a home of rare personal expression. There are things here you simply cannot purchase from a decorator's showroom: the plaster bust of a much-loved stallion that is the centerpiece of the barn entrance hall, the tabletops filled with family photos, the hand-painted murals in the children's nursery. Like the songs he sings, this place has a way of making one fall into a lovely state of mellow.

Photography: John Coulter, L. David Dwinell and Max Eckert.

Beaver Dam Farms was presented in Unique Homes by Gerry Whitworth and Margie Hancock of Coldwell Banker Upchurch Realty, Athens, Georgia.

OPPOSITE: *A marble entry lobby with custom-designed ceiling and inlaid wooden floor welcomes visitors to one of the most unusual barns in the world.* TOP: *Designed in the same architectural style as the main house, the barn is a functional yet compellingly attractive complex of more than 72,000 square feet. It includes 60 custom-built stalls, tack rooms, a therapeutic whirlpool for the conditioning of horses, executive offices, a fully equipped exercise room, and three spacious apartments including a luxurious guest suite.* ABOVE: *Also located in the main barn complex is a magnificent show arena, surrounded by a hand-wrought brass rail.*

An Old World PERSPECTIVE

Château Thal

In Belgium, near the German town of Aachen

LEFT: *Trompe l'oeil walls created by Rainer Maria Latzke and fine paneling add to the warm ambience in the parlor.*
ABOVE: *Château Thal sits majestically on more than 17 park-like acres complete with extensive lawns, towering trees, footpaths and a lily pond.*

When Rainer Maria Latzke first encountered Château Thal in 1984, generations of accumulated dust and neglect could in no way mask this sleeping beauty rimmed by the forests, heath lands, streams and lakes of the northern Ardennes. The electrical age may have long since come to the modern world, but clearly not to this castle-like manor built by Seigneur de Grand Ry in 1750. "After we had our first look," recalls the German-born artist, then in his thirties, "my wife and I turned to one another and tried to recall if we'd even seen a bath-room inside." This was the beginning of a reconstruction which would last three full years, employ more than 70 craftspersons and artists, and result in one of the most magical revivals of an ancient home ever attempted.

In a romantic park of grassy lawns and footpaths, towering hardwoods and a secluded lily pond, the château stands today much as it appeared when the young Wolfgang Amadeus Mozart visited the Grand Rys over two centuries ago. On occasion, herds of cows still lazily graze their way across the landscape; and 15 minutes away, in Germany, the medieval spa town of Aachen

CHARACTERISTICS

PROPERTY SIZE: 17½ acres.

ARCHITECTURAL STYLE: European stone manor.

WHEN BUILT/RENOVATED: Built in 1750. Thoroughly restored in the 1980s.

NUMBER OF ROOMS: 35.

SQUARE FOOTAGE: 11,000.

NUMBER OF BEDROOMS: 20.

OUTBUILDINGS: Summerhouse located beside a secluded lily pond.

DISTINCTIVE ARCHITECTURAL DETAILS: Important collection of antiques, cut-glass chandeliers, parquet and marble floors, hand-fashioned stucco ornamentation and the owner's own trompe l'oeil architectural motifs and frescoes throughout.

SPECIAL APPOINTMENTS AND/OR AMENITIES: Now in the planning stages is an on-site spa facility with pool, steam bath, whirlpool, sauna and fitness center.

ADDITIONAL HIGHLIGHTS: Situated between Brussels, Cologne and Dusseldorf, this romantic Belgian castle is surrounded by parklands with extensive lawns and footpaths, a variety of ancient hard-woods, entertaining terraces and a pond.

LEFT: *The dramatic effect of the main staircase is heightened by the use of trompe l'oeil paintings on the walls and ceiling.* BELOW: *Displaying a host of classic old world appointments is the great hall, which opens out to the idyllic park-like setting.*

seems to linger in a time when it served as Charlemagne's imperial city. As is the story with any great fairy tale, though, distinguishing fact from illusion is the great fascination of Château Thal, for here Rainer Maria Latzke has created a residence where each room serves as a threshold to an incredible journey.

Though he studied art extensively in Dusseldorf under avant-gardist Joseph Beuys, Rainer's artistic sensibilities were, from the onset, clearly more akin to Tiepolo and the 18th century. One look inside the 35-room château affirms why his fellow students in Germany often exclaimed, "Rainer, you're two centuries too late!"

The ceiling of the first-floor entrance hall is an allegorical fresco: three Herculean figures (including a

ABOVE: *The dining room includes one of the château's many elegant fireplaces.* LEFT: *Fragments found in the attic provided the clue to the recreation of this Moorish chamber. Into this fanciful bedroom, Latzke discreetly integrated such modern conveniences as a stereo system, a concealed television and bar.*

likeness of Rainer's brother) holding tight to a lamp so that it will not fall on anyone below, with a surround of dinosaurs adding further tension to the scene. Upstairs, the owner turned walls into windows with fabulous trompe l'oeil motifs: a hunt scene straight out of the Black Forest in a handsomely paneled parlor, Renaissance gardens complete with columns and balustrades in the master bath, and, in the library, the image of a young lad in period dress overlooking the château and its grounds as they appeared in the 1790s.

Where he has not stretched the boundaries of his 11,000-square-foot castle through his own classical murals, Rainer Latzke has masterfully revived the original design. "The greatest challenge in this renovation was to make everything up-to-date, from modern plumbing and heating to computerized communications, without harming the lustrous original floors, antique plasterwork, stucco ornamentation and priceless fittings."

In the extensive reconstruction of Château Thal, many clues of 18th century life here were unearthed, but none more alluring than the remnants of a bedroom straight out of Scheherazade. Rainer's commissions at the time for Arabian royalty provided all the prompting he needed to recreate this Moorish sanctuary complete with gilded arabesques, lapis-colored fabrics, repeated papyrus patterns and fabulous beasts shining out of the depths of onion-colored paneling. "This is my tent in the Arabian desert...my escape," explains the owner, who admits he has left nothing to the imagination, with the possible exception of a jeweled harem awaiting at bedside.

Having completed this project along with several world-class hotels and a major commission for Daimler-Benz, Rainer Maria Latzke is taking some time out on the beaches of Malibu with his wife and their three children, one of whom was born at Château Thal. For a man who has devoted his career to creating illusion by transforming flat surfaces into fantastic dimensions, his vision remains surprisingly grounded. "Twenty years from now I hope I'll have more time to enjoy music and golf. I also hope I'll still be painting." One thing is certain in today's often illusionary world: His craft is timeless.

Photography by Ralph Bremen.

Château Thal was presented in Unique Homes by Classics International, Malibu, California.

OPPOSITE: *Latzke's trompe l'oeil artistry even embellishes the spacious master bathroom.* LEFT: *Adjacent to the château is a lovely terrace, perfect for an alfresco breakfast on a summer morning.* BELOW: *The front facade of Château Thal viewed in the evening.*

A Screen Gem

Pasadena, California

LEFT: *Designed by noted architects Marston and VanPelt nearly 80 years ago for railroad scion William Kennon Jewett, this classic residence is one of Pasadena's finest estate homes. Over the past six decades, it has appeared in countless movies, television shows and commercials, and is probably best known as the Carrington mansion on the TV series "Dynasty."* ABOVE: *A wraparound staircase is the focal point of the grand entry hall.*

When Coleman and Jane Morton purchased the one-time residence of railroad scion William Kennon Jewett in 1957, it was clearly not with the intention of living in an enormous Palladian villa dating back to 1915. They envisioned all the modern comforts of a streamlined contemporary home, and recruited architects to draw up the necessary plans for one which would replace the existing three-story Jewett mansion built by Sylvester Marston and Garrett VanPelt. "The designs were simply not within our budget," explains the now-retired Coleman Morton, "and thank God!" After 35 years at this landmark Pasadena estate, their only regret is that the time has come to scale down a bit.

The two and one-half-acre property is immediately recognized by anyone who has spent more than an evening in front of the television. Here Ringo Starr was featured in a commercial for Oldsmobile, George Burns promoted Teledyne, O.J. Simpson sold the world on Hertz, and Godzilla extolled the taste of Bud Lite. Here, too, Hollywood found a ready-made set for scenes from "The Twilight Zone," "Matlock," "The A-Team,"

"Charlie's Angels," "Murder She Wrote" and some four dozen other popular shows. Movie credits range from the Marx Brothers' "Duck Soup" to the award-winning "Terms of Endearment." But it was the long-running dramatic series "Dynasty" that clearly made the home a star. Looking out onto the reflecting pool where Joan Collins and Linda Evans made waves in the cat fight of the decade, Coleman Morton brings us back into the real world. "If you've spent any time watching a show being taped, you know it really isn't that thrilling, and every shot seems to take forever."

From the tree-lined 100-foot drive approaching the three-story villa on Arden Road, there's a somewhat incongruous glimpse of the state flag of Maryland flying over the hipped Spanish tile rooftop. Explains Jane Morton: "My father was a graduate of the Naval Academy, at age 16 I was the Chaplain's secretary, Coleman and I were married there, and our first child was born there—in fact, it was the first baby ever delivered at the U.S. Naval Academy Hospital." Five children and 12 grandchildren later, their home is now filled with family portraits, works by one of their artist-daugh-

ABOVE: *A marble fireplace with ornate woodwork, French doors, handsome moldings and decorative plasterwork patterning on the ceiling create an atmosphere of classic old world elegance in the formal living room.* OPPOSITE TOP: *The parlor's cast ceiling decoration in a floral medallion style and intricately carved fireplace are indicative of the impeccable detail found throughout the home.* OPPOSITE BOTTOM: *Regal-sized public rooms, such as the formal dining room seen here, easily accommodate entertaining on a grand scale.*

🏛 𝒞HARACTERISTICS

PROPERTY SIZE: Approximately two and one-half acres.

ARCHITECTURAL STYLE: Palladian villa.

WHEN BUILT/RENOVATED: Built in 1915; continuous upgrades over the past 35 years.

NUMBER OF ROOMS: 18.

SQUARE FOOTAGE: 12,000.

NUMBER OF BEDROOMS: Nine.

OUTBUILDINGS: Five-car detached garage.

DISTINCTIVE ARCHITECTURAL DETAILS: Cast floral ceiling medallions, formal Ionic columns, marble floors, seven fireplaces, glass and iron gated entry, monumental wraparound staircase, tray ceilings, regal old world appointments throughout.

SPECIAL APPOINTMENTS AND/OR AMENITIES: Large kitchen with multiple pantries to facilitate entertaining, elevator, circular brick courtyard, swimming pool, tennis court, reflecting pool, koi pond, gazebo, sculpture gardens.

ADDITIONAL HIGHLIGHTS: This widely recognized home has provided a backdrop for countless Hollywood motion pictures and television shows, including Alfred Hitchcock's "Dark Mirror," Eddie Murphy's "Distinguished Gentleman," various episodes of "Falcon Crest," "Fantasy Island" and "Highway to Heaven"; plus commercials promoting Mercedes Benz, 7-Up, Georgio and Ralph Lauren, among others. It is most often recognized as the "Dynasty House" from the popular TV series featuring Linda Evans, Joan Collins and John Forsythe.

ters, garden bouquets which Jane loves to arrange herself, and 35 years of feel-good memories.

The Morton's have a humble and often humorous side that seems to make the austerity of the home disappear. Framed by classical statuary and formal gardens, the brick-paved motor court approaches a facade and columned portico decked out in Palladian ornament. Unusual Aztec-looking figures rise amid the waters of the entry fountain, and when asked about their origin, Mr. Morton has a good laugh. "I like to tell people these are pre-Columbian treasures, but actually they're pieces we discovered by a recent graduate student at the Otis Art Institute."

Inside the 18-room, 12,000-square-foot villa, it's easy to understand why Jane Morton says she's "so proud to show it off." The monumental wraparound staircase in the grand entry hall immediately establishes a sense of lavish scale and appointment. Principal rooms are filled with marble floors, cast floral ceiling medallions, Ionic columns, silvery sconces, French doors and elaborately carved fireplaces. Multiple pantries, a private elevator, the glassed-in music room and lower-level billiards parlor are but a few of the old world privileges. The tennis

ABOVE: *A terrace running the length of the house provides an ideal vantage point for viewing matches on the tennis court.* RIGHT: *Lush landscaping and mature trees form a sylvan backdrop for the swimming pool and reflecting pool, framed here by one of the loggia's columned arches. Sculpture gardens and a koi pond are also featured on the nearly two and one-half-acre grounds.*

court and swimming pool are newer complements to the decades-old gardens. And the exquisite archways, wrought iron and glass doors, and multi-paned windows overlook a scene that has only become more beautiful with every generation. This may be one of the most recognized houses in America, but it's not likely you'll ever see it from the road.

The Morton's have brought an inescapable sense of peace to this home; a calm which didn't always exist. The second Mrs. Jewett is said to have raised her glass to Hitler at a dinner party in the early 1940s, instantly becoming the disgrace of the community. A later owner, a Las Vegas developer, ended up abandoning his wife in the 18-room house, leaving the woman virtually penniless and without a piece of furniture. Coleman Morton sounds almost apologetic when he says he can't recall any alarming incident, except perhaps the day John McEnroe was starring in a commercial being filmed on the tennis court. "It was at the time McEnroe was trying to turn his courtside reputation around and become something more of a gentleman. I approached him and said, 'I'd like to meet the new Mr. McEnroe.' Well, I

guess he didn't find that humorous at all."

From Alfred Hitchcock and Liberace to Bo Derek and Billy Crystal, the Morton's' home has hosted more luminaries over the years than any back lot at MGM or Universal combined. But for Jane Morton, the biggest thrill is an annual event that involves all 20-odd members of the family—and there's not a star, soundman or camera in sight. "For 35 years everyone has come here for Christmas, staying through the Tournament of Roses Parade." (Their property abuts Tournament Park, the original terminus of the parade). "The house just seems to open up to everyone, making us all feel comfortable and happy in being together," says Jane.

Her husband concludes, "Next Christmas we may be in closer quarters, but I'm sure we'll all manage to be together."

Photography by Nick Springett.

This estate was presented in Unique Homes by Carol Thomson of Podley Caughey & Doan Realtors®, Pasadena, California.

Oak Knoll

Mill Neck, Long Island, New York

The setting is one that would have turned the Gatsby green. Just across the valley is the big old house Alfred Vanderbilt (and later Sonny Whitney) occupied. From a grand terrace banked by elegant balustrades, verdant lands slope down to Oyster Bay where the view stretches out to Long Island Sound and the Connecticut coast. Amid placid reflecting pools and fountains, classical statuary and formal gardens, the Italianate villa rises to the occasion on 18 acres of private grounds secured behind Romanesque gates. It's one of those rare homes where architectural integrity is surpassed only by the great care given to the place by its owners throughout time.

Built in 1916-1918 by Delano & Aldrich for Goodrich Rubber Company chairman Bertram Work, Oak Knoll is named for the largest white oak on Long Island. One has a great view of this mighty specimen from the master

OPPOSITE: *The elegant sun room opens to both a terrace and a formal garden.* ABOVE: *Mirrored in one of the property's two reflecting pools, the main residence is reminiscent of a grand Italian villa. Manicured landscaping further heightens the old world ambience of the estate.*

bedroom, part of a multi-room suite incorporating a private inner study, two baths, walk-in closets, a large terrace and a total of three fireplaces. Mr. Work lived on the property until his death a decade or so later, at which time title passed to his son. In 1966, Mr. and Mrs. Bronson Trevor purchased Oak Knoll from the only other previous owners, Mrs. Trevor's parents. Thus, this Gold Coast treasure has been home to only two families since its creation nearly 80 years ago. With the exception of contemporary mechanical systems, a new roof, modern elevator with telephone, and upgrades in the name of comfort, nothing much has changed.

Indeed the house has its imposing aspects, the 40- by 60-foot drawing room paneled in book-matched English walnut among them. (This backdrop was recently photo-shoot material for print promotions by Ralph Lauren and Victoria's Secret.) Occasionally there are touches of whimsy as well, including the walls of the breakfast room painted with original frescoes by Gardner Hale. Mr. Trevor describes the scene as "mostly flora and fauna. A monkey is pulling on a bird's tail in one corner, and the

OPPOSITE: *Generously proportioned to accommodate grand-scale gatherings, the drawing room sets a formal tone with its book-matched English walnut paneling, high ceiling, beautifully crafted moldings and woodwork, and handsome fireplace.* ABOVE: *Complete with its own fireplace, the lounge area of the ladies' powder room offers a decidedly European ambience.*

bird is pecking at the monkey's tail in another." Though the owners have removed the big bar where Work would entertain his cronies, they kept his original gun cabinet, which is why the gentleman's washroom on the main floor is often referred to as the "gun room." There is also a ladies' powder room featuring a lounge area with fireplace.

The dining room in which Mrs. Trevor seats 24 for dinner is fit for elegant evening dress and candlelight with its marble floor and a fireplace flanked by oil landscapes in the Flemish style. The attendant kitchen houses two ranges, two dishwashers and two refrigerator/freezers along with a mammoth walk-in silver safe. Another kitchen facility is found on the third floor within a staff wing containing five maid's bedrooms.

Outdoors, from a charming gazebo crowned by a frescoed ceiling, one has a view of a pergola reminiscent of a European grape arbor. Anyone who has seen "Godfather III" might well recognize the structure. Mr. Trevor maintains there wasn't much excitement during the two or three days the movie crew was at Oak Knoll. "I was simply grateful they didn't burn the place down!" From here, there is also a splendid overlook to the double row of

established Linden trees bordering the gardens. With a terrace, balcony or veranda off nearly every room, the proportions seem to go on and on.

Mr. Trevor, once an oil man and later the largest spinach farmer on the eastern seaboard, and at one time the supplier of potatoes to Schraffts ("before they started using the powdered version"), has a wit and frankness that remains unfettered by the impressiveness of his home of nearly 30 years. "My favorite space in the house? The master bedroom. It has the big television." And when asked what he'll miss most about the place, he answers, "The ambience...not the bills."

It is this very ambience that the Trevors have preserved and protected during their time at Oak Knoll, ensuring that Bertram Work's Italian villa will continue to grow more exquisite with each passing generation.

Photography by Michael Forester.

Oak Knoll was presented in Unique Homes by Caroline Salas, The Prudential Long Island Realty, Locust Valley, New York.

☖ CHARACTERISTICS

PROPERTY SIZE: 18 acres overlooking Oyster Bay Harbor.

ARCHITECTURAL STYLE: Italian-style villa designed by Delano & Aldrich.

WHEN BUILT/RENOVATED: Built in 1916 and continually upgraded.

NUMBER OF ROOMS: Approximately 20.

NUMBER OF BEDROOMS: Eight (exclusive of staff).

NUMBER OF BATHS: Six (exclusive of staff).

OUTBUILDINGS: Three-bedroom caretaker's cottage with greenhouse, separate garage with apartment and barn, rental cottage, gazebo with frescoed ceiling, and pergola featured in "Godfather III."

DISTINCTIVE ARCHITECTURAL DETAILS: Hand-carved moldings, oak parquet floors, French doors, book-matched English walnut paneling, French oak paneling, marble floors and fireplaces, original walls painted by Gardner Hale, grand marble staircase with overhead skylight.

SPECIAL APPOINTMENTS AND/OR AMENITIES: Master suite with two bedrooms, two baths, private inner study and a total of three fireplaces. Balconies, terraces and verandas throughout. Two reflecting pools and statuary amid formal gardens, specimen trees, lawns and fountains. New elevator, new roof, modernized electrical and climate control systems. Five-bedroom staff suite in main house.

OPPOSITE: *A fitting backdrop for formal occasions, the baronial dining room is appointed with flooring of polished marble, a marble fireplace and original oil landscapes inset into the walls.* ABOVE: *French oak paneling adorns the walls of the library, also featuring recessed bookcases and a marble fireplace.*

The Tower of Lethendy at Meikleour

Perthshire, Scotland

In the scenic Tay Valley, about 15 miles from Perth, stands a fairy tale house where it's easy to envision Rapunzel letting down her hair. With portions dating back to the 1500s, it's a home that has been gabled and turreted to perfection. The moat no longer stands guard over this keep; in its place are 200-year-old walnut, beech, sycamore and Douglas fir trees providing a more natural shelter. Within various brick-walled gardens are emerald lawns, four seasons of flower beds and herbaceous borders. To the south is a croquet lawn with small stone pond and fountain. To the east is the swimming pool with its accompanying summer house. A rockery—a pastoral spot for alpine beds and a water garden—and lily ponds are also featured. There's a romance to the place that comes alive with the first glimpse of this castle and its grounds.

Originally built as a fortified tower house or keep, Tower of Lethendy was largely reconstructed in 1855 in the prevailing Scottish baronial style, though many elements of its original form remain, including the six-foot-thick walls in the billiard room and the now-legendary tombstones which

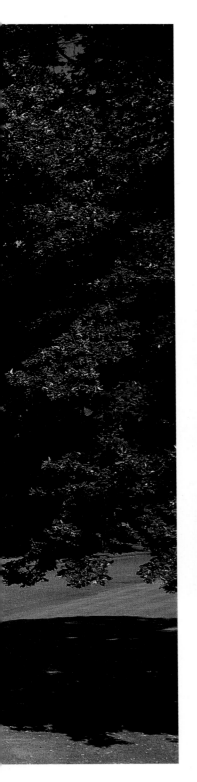

ABOVE: *The Tower of Lethendy as it appears today. Extensive additions made to the 16th century structure in 1885 were done in the same red sandstone as the original tower.* TOP RIGHT: *One of the property's most unusual and entertaining features is the private golf course situated literally a matter of yards from the front door.* BOTTOM RIGHT: *Hedges and cut cypress trees form a natural screen for the heated kidney-shaped pool.*

RIGHT: *Magnificent gardens and specimen trees add to the fairy tale qualities of this enchanting castle.* OPPOSITE TOP AND BOTTOM: *Traditional plasterwork, classic wood paneling and handsome fireplaces are among the appointments gracing the reception rooms. Extensive refurbishing and modernization were carried out in the 1970s, and today the home is in excellent condition throughout.*

the 16th century laborers pilfered from a nearby cemetery. "I suppose the workmen were just lazy," remarks the owner. "They saw stones of just the proper dimension in the graveyard and the rest is history." The tombstones, he adds, date back to the 10th or 11th century.

When asked if there were ghosts in the house, the current owner responded, "Not that I've met yet. If they are here, they seem to ignore me." He admits, however, that one or two overnight guests have appeared a bit wide-eyed the next morning—both here and at another property the family owns, an old abbey dating back some 900 years.

In the early 1970s, the home again underwent extensive refurbishing and modernization, and its condition continues to be excellent. The three-story interior is characterized by traditional plasterwork and wood paneling, baronial arches and vaulted ceilings, plus an assortment of modern comforts rarely seen in a house dating back to Shakespeare's day. The office is fully computerized with the latest communications systems. The kitchen is equipped for catering on a grand scale, though there remain some old world delights such as the dumbwaiter (now electric) to the pantry and an adjoining game larder. The owner's mirrored exercise room

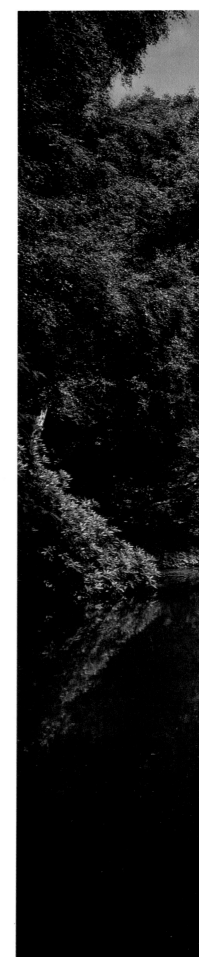

𝒞HARACTERISTICS

PROPERTY SIZE: Approximately 38 acres.

ARCHITECTURAL STYLE: 16th century keep reconstructed in 1885 in the Scottish baronial style.

WHEN BUILT/RENOVATED: Built circa 1570; substantial additions/restorations in 19th and 20th centuries.

NUMBER OF ROOMS: Approximately 20.

NUMBER OF BEDROOMS: Eight suites plus a staff flat.

OUTBUILDINGS: Four cottages and a summerhouse.

DISTINCTIVE ARCHITECTURAL DETAILS: Built of red sandstone with crow-stepped gables, turrets and conical as well as pitched slate rooflines.

SPECIAL APPOINTMENTS AND/OR AMENITIES: 18-hole golf course, all-weather tennis court, heated pool with cabana facilities, two miles of salmon fishing rights on River Tay, plus outstanding gardens and grounds. Interior highlights include a gymnasium with sauna and a computerized office. A historic Scottish barony title is included with the property and will be conveyed to the new owner at the time of sale.

includes a sauna, rowing machine, exercise bicycle and various other workout devices.

Tower of Lethendy is situated in a region world-famous for golf; the courses at Gleneagles, St. Andrews and Carnoustie are all within a 30-minute drive. However, the owners and their guests prefer the course that's right outside the front door. Apart from Balmoral, this is probably the only other privately owned golf course in Scotland. With six well-contoured greens and seven tees, it's played as an 18-hole course from different angles with a par of 54. "We've enjoyed many golfing competitions here," says the owner, adding that Ben Crenshaw currently holds the course record at Lethendy with a score of one under par. The home game takes on a very relaxed pace as martinis are served on the sixth, twelfth and eighteenth holes—often accompanied by smoked salmon sandwiches.

In fact, one is hard-pressed not to run into salmon in one form or another during their stay here. The River Tay offers the finest salmon fishing in the world, and conveyed with this property are two miles of fishing rights on the Lower Middle Tay. From mid-January until well into October, two beats are fished easily from both banks, by wading or by boat. With a bag of over 330

OPPOSITE: *The old world meets the new in the handsomely paneled office, complete with computerized telephone system and facsimile equipment.* LEFT: *The glen, which is said to have been part of the tower's original moat, runs south to a pond, the slopes of which are home to the rockery and water garden.* BELOW: *Included with the property are superb salmon fishing rights on the Delvine and Kercock beats of the River Tay.*

salmon in 1992, there seems to be no shortage of catches in the 11- to 13-pound range. The owner laughs, "When we're short on time I can send a gillie out to the river. When all looks well, he'll raise a flag I can spot from the house, and then I know it's time to fish!" Peerage does have its privileges.

Finally, as part of a feudal legacy, each owner since the original founder of the Tower of Lethendy—a Sir David Herron of Drumlochy—has inherited an ancient Scottish barony title. It is a tradition which continues still today. For over 400 years the estate has been the gem of Scotland's most panoramic countryside, located at the threshold to the Highlands, about 60 miles from Edinburgh. "At night," concludes the owner, "when you come down the drive toward the main house and it's all lit from within, it's a scene out of "Cinderella." It's absolutely beautiful."

Photography by John Dewar.

The Tower of Lethendy was presented in Unique Homes by Knight Frank & Rutley International, Edinburgh, Scotland.

An English
Manor Reborn

Lake Forest, Illinois

In 1932, *Architectural Digest* featured the dining room, a 400-square-foot fantasy of chinoiserie style with black and white marble floors, eight French doors and a medieval bay of leaded and stained glass windows. No doubt the magazine was chattiest about the celadon green radiator cover ornamented with floral designs and marbleized on the top in black and green. The feature appeared a few years after one-time owner John Jelke (heir to the "Good Luck" margarine fortune) had the house expanded by Mayo & Mayo. In a more recent magazine article, the story focused on the current residents of this Lake Forest manor, now experts in the art of making a landmark most livable.

From the onset they had wanted a big, formal house, but also a place where kids could be kids and you could put your feet up on the coffee table. The large marble fountain in the now-famous dining room housed the children's goldfish until the family cat joined in the fun. Sometime later, during a sit-down dinner for over one hundred people, the band played as guests danced the

ABOVE: *The manor home as it appears today. It was originally designed by Ernest K. Mayo, a member of the Royal Institute of British Architects, and built in 1916-17; then dramatically expanded a decade later under the direction of Mayo & Mayo, by then a nationally respected firm with a number of major clients on the North Shore.*
TOP RIGHT: *The symmetry and tranquility of the gardens are reminiscent of an English park.*
BOTTOM RIGHT: *French doors, medieval bays and leaded and stained glass windows are found throughout the expansive 15-room home.*

OPPOSITE: *A barrel-vaulted ceiling crowns the manor's 27-foot-long entry hall.* ABOVE: *Numerous sets of French doors open the formal dining room —scene of many parties and gatherings over the years—to the terrace.* LEFT: *It is believed that the exquisite paneling and pediments, doors and dentil moldings in the living room were carved by Highwood craftsmen who came from Italy. The work of these talented artisans can be seen in the interior embellishments of many a North Shore estate home.*

night away on the marble floor. Recalls the lady of the house, "The drummer was in the empty fountain."

Getting an aging manor house that had been built in 1917 in shape for modern living was not all laughs, though. The wife, a gold- and silversmith, stripped and refinished the rosewood armoire in the dining room along with virtually all of the original brass throughout the 15-room home. In 1979, the owners added an over-sized three-car garage, and in 1983, remodeled the kitchen and butler's pantry. By then their initial over-whelming concerns about the house (practicality, liv-ability, etc.) were a distant memory.

In the house, where "no ways" turned into "why nots," the owners have left much of the original detail intact: the barrel-vaulted plaster ceiling and wrought iron stair railing in the 27-foot entry hall, the beamed oak library with its "secret staircase" to one of the upstairs hallways, and the carved panel moldings and fabulous pediments in the living room, which opens through five pairs of doors to the gardens. It is believed much of the exquisite pine woodwork was done by Highwood craftsmen who came from Italy in the early 1900s and embellished many of the more lavish North Shore estates of the period.

The design and dimension of each of the public rooms

RIGHT: *Listed on the National Register of Historic Places, the home possesses a stateliness and formality of architecture one might come across in the English countryside.* OPPOSITE TOP: *In the library, the beamed ceiling, fireplace and leaded glass windows suggest the graciousness of another era. Hidden behind one of the room's many bookshelves is a secret staircase that leads to an upstairs hallway.* OPPOSITE BOTTOM: *The rear facade of the home as viewed from one of the gardens.*

suggest a host of possibilities for living, entertaining and leisure. The dining room has provided an elegant backdrop for church teas, private parties and receptions for the Lake Forest Symphony. The living room is both recital hall and elegant retreat, with a Steinway piano at one end, and an assortment of beautiful furnishings and oriental rugs at the other. Downstairs are the wine cellar, darkroom and workshop; upstairs are seven family bedrooms and baths.

Originally designed by Ernest K. Mayo, a member of the Royal Institute of British Architects, and first occupied by an internationally known importer, the English country manor continues to instill a sense of connoisseurship. In the house where, according to the owners, "even the gutters are signed," the husband and wife display their own collection of antiques and artifacts collected in their travels over the years. An oil painting on the east wall of the dining room is thought to be a 17th century portrait of Edward Winslow, governor of the Plymouth Colony. The pine-paneled living room pro-

vides a formal backdrop for pre-Columbian pieces. A Peruvian burial cloth and a spear and shield from Africa are on view in the den. Both husband and wife steer away from decorators; their preference for a more individual statement is very much in evidence.

The owners have revived their North Shore residence with unique energy and style while remaining ever-mindful of its National Register status. Nowhere in the home does one encounter that "what can we get away with" look. Approximately two park-like acres of formal English gardens and a deeply wooded ravine make the manor complete. It's private, established and without pretense. It all just seems to belong here.

Photography by Michael J. Kardas.

This classic North Shore manor was presented in Unique Homes by Ned Skae, The Prudential Preferred Properties, Lake Forest, Illinois.

🏛 CHARACTERISTICS

PROPERTY SIZE: Approximately two acres.

ARCHITECTURAL STYLE: English country manor.

WHEN BUILT/RENOVATED: Built in 1916-17, with major additions a decade later; remodeled and expanded 1979-1983 by present owners.

NUMBER OF ROOMS: 15.

NUMBER OF BEDROOMS: Seven.

NUMBER OF BATHS: Seven and one-half.

DISTINCTIVE ARCHITECTURAL DETAILS: Custom moldings, solid brass hardware and hardwood floors throughout, carved paneling in living room, leaded and stained glass windows, 10- and 12-foot ceilings, hand-painted tiles in modern kitchen, huge oak doors and beamed ceiling in library, marble floor and fountain in dining room.

SPECIAL APPOINTMENTS AND/OR AMENITIES: Elevator in grand reception hall, two game rooms on third floor, basement wine cellar and darkroom, five fireplaces. Many modern built-ins including some central air conditioning, security system and fire alarm. Three staff bedrooms with bath.

ADDITIONAL HIGHLIGHTS: A National Register home on park-like grounds encompassing large formal gardens and a heavily wooded ravine. Located within a 30-minute drive of O'Hare International Airport.

Floralyn

Lattingtown, Long Island, New York

Their escape from the city is a botanical dream of nearly 20 acres on Long Island's North Shore; these are grounds firmly rooted in the old farm-estates of the 18th century, with the 200-year-old trees and gardens listed among the most exquisite in America. They divide their time between this property and residences in Manhattan and Belgium. But, when springtime comes—rhododendrons, azaleas, irises, herbaceous borders and cutting gardens all in bloom—the owners of Floralyn admit that it's hard to be

any place other than their celebrated estate in the heart of the delightful village of Lattingtown.

Built before 1873, the one-time Quaker farmhouse is now an expanded and lovingly restored ideal of the English country manor, given new life by its owners with the help of interior designer Thomas Britt and English landscape architect Adèle Mitchell. For four years, the husband claims, there were painters literally living in the house, woodwork being stripped, trees being planted and a west wing larger than most houses being added on.

OPPOSITE: *The living room evokes a formal mood with its marble fireplace, random-width pegged flooring, raised carved paneling and crown moldings. French doors to the covered bluestone terrace and an elevator to the master suite are also found in this room.* TOP: *The front façade of the main house at Floralyn.* ABOVE: *Decorated in the Edwardian style, the sitting room of the master suite features a hand-carved mantel.*

Though from the start, he adds, there was "a rightness to the place in its quality, age and majesty." Today, looking out from a side window in the master bedroom to a view of pink rose gardens, structured hedges and a canopy of towering trees, he says, "It gives me a lot of pleasure to simply be here."

Adèle Mitchell, recommended to the owners by a friend, was brought onto the scene in 1988 to refine the lavishly planned layout of grounds which were originally established by another English landscape designer, Noel Chamberlain, back in the 1920s. Chamberlain's plan included an eclectic mix of 19th century Italian and French statuary, a water garden, steps and terraces descending from the rear facade, and parterre-like beds mirroring the classical symmetry of the home itself.

In a recent article on "Floralyn" in *House and Garden*, Ms. Mitchell, who likes to plan gardens as if they were sets for a play, commented: "You need entrances and exits so the players don't trip over one another." Indeed, her stage here is a prolific one and clearly well nurtured by the estate's gardener-in-residence for the past 20 years or so. Since the current owners purchased the property in 1984, another 100 trees have been added to the sylvan landscape.

OPPOSITE: *In the large entrance foyer, exquisite dentil moldings and a free-standing circular staircase establish a level of elegance that is carried throughout the formal areas of the home.* ABOVE: *Paneling carved by artisans who worked on the ocean liner "Mauritania" is one of the highlights of the library/morning room.* LEFT: *An Adam-style mantel containing white marble from England's Edenthorpe Hall, raised panel wainscoting and crown moldings characterize the banquet-size formal dining room.*

 CHARACTERISTICS

PROPERTY SIZE: 19 park-like acres.

ARCHITECTURAL STYLE: Colonial Revival.

WHEN BUILT/RENOVATED: House dates to the 1870s; east wing added in 1929; west wing added in 1986. House also thoroughly renovated in 1986.

SQUARE FOOTAGE: 12,000.

OUTBUILDINGS: Two- bedroom guest house, pool house, teahouse, five-car garage with caretaker's quarters, machine barn, greenhouse and gazebo.

DISTINCTIVE ARCHITECTURAL DETAILS: Random-width pegged floors, paneling by artisans who worked on the "Mauritania," crown moldings, raised panel wainscoting, carved leaf moldings, seven fireplaces.

SPECIAL APPOINTMENTS AND/OR AMENITIES: "Telephone room" with wet bar and stereo system, bluestone terrace, gourmet kitchen, butler's pantry and breakfast room, elevator to master suite, media room, indoor pool and exercise room.

ADDITIONAL HIGHLIGHTS: This important estate has meticulously planned grounds with formal and cutting gardens, rose and vegetable gardens, a goldfish pond, azalea walk, tennis court with gazebo, swimming pool and important statuary.

When first moving in, however, the owners' attention was on a 19th century home that was both a treasure chest of wonderful finds as well as a Pandora's box of exhaustive challenges. There was the morning room, with paneled walls crafted by the same artisans who had done woodwork on the ocean liner "Mauritania," and the dining room, displaying a mantel with marble from Edenthorpe Hall. There was also the living room, in which the stripping down of its elegant oak panels revealed mismatched sections where some of the old wood had been replaced. "Then we began the faux bois process of making it all look original once again," says the man of the house. "Today you really can't tell what's been replaced." Designer Tom Britt also recalls the gallons of bleach used to remove the dark brown finish in the library. As luck would have it, some of the wood had aged differently, and so they stained and bleached once again.

Today, "Floralyn" is sun-drenched, filled with French doors, flowers and chintz, and another 5,000 square feet grander after the addition of a west wing that looks like it's belonged forever. When asked if any of their younger children or guests have ever become lost in the house that now measures some 12,000 square feet, the owner answers, with a hint of reluctance and no shortage of humor: "No. They always seem to find their way to the kitchen!" It's a beautiful space with glass-doored pine

OPPOSITE: *With 19 private, superbly landscaped acres, an impeccable manor home rich in old world detail, a host of outbuildings, and an endless list of superior appointments and amenities, Floralyn is undoubtedly one of the North Shore's premier properties. It is comparable in terms of the quality of its architecture and its grounds to renowned Old Westbury Gardens.* LEFT: *The chamber of the master suite is a spacious, light-filled room graciously adorned with carved leaf moldings and an Adamstyle marble mantel.*

cabinets, copper sink, center island and flower arranging area, joined by a breakfast room as well as a butler's pantry which leads into the formal dining room.

In the newly built wing there is the Corinthian exercise room with its lap pool, a second-floor apartment with living room, kitchen and two bedrooms, and stairs leading to the playroom, private office, exercise room and a health room with Jacuzzi tub, steam bath and sauna. Beyond the columned bluestone terrace is a picturesque country cottage that serves as the guest house, a pool house with teahouse wing, and a detached five-car garage with caretaker's quarters above.

Off in a quiet corner of the sunken garden, an antique lead statue of a woman directs her gaze upon bearded irises and oriental poppies touched with a brushstroke of crimson. Slightly above her line of vision is the birdhouse, a tiny replica of the main house at Floralyn made for the current owners by their estate superintendent. "There was another miniature version of the house here," explains the owner, "but it was old and in need of repair. Now we have a bigger and more beautiful place where the birds may come home."

Photography by Jeffrey Heatley.

Floralyn was presented in Unique Homes by the firm of Douglas Elliman-Jane Hayes, Locust Valley, New York. Co-exclusive brokers for the property are Kevin Daigh of Douglas Elliman-Jane Hayes and Bonnie Devendorf of Daniel Gale Associates, Locust Valley, New York.

A Panoramic
PERSPECTIVE

1049 Fifth Avenue

New York City

Fifth Avenue has always been the choice of those for whom money is no object. Keeping good company with its next-door neighbor, the last and loveliest of the Vanderbilt mansions at Fifth Avenue and 86th Street, is the 23-story condominium building that's being hailed by many as the city's most elegant: 1049 Fifth Avenue. The predominant focus is Manhattan's 843-acre garden, Central Park. Steps away are the Guggenheim, Cooper Hewitt and Metropolitan Museums, plus shops, galleries, schools and restaurants that have catered to New York's first families for generations. Jack Heller, the 37-year-old developer of 1049 Fifth Avenue, says he does his best to avoid the term "luxury" when it comes to his building. It really doesn't need to be mentioned in this neighborhood. It's understood.

Once known as the Adams Hotel, the 1928 structure first

captured Heller's eye in the winter of 1988. It was the last available great social register address, and at a time when, due to downturns in the market, most of his competitors were putting out fires, Jack Heller was keeping cool with plans for converting the old hotel into one of New York's greatest landmark buildings. "There's a tremendous amount of money around the world that desperately needs a home," he said in a recent interview with *Business Age* magazine. At 1049 Fifth Avenue, he made that home happen.

A 32-page brochure for the now-completed building describes the 45 condominium residences as formal, understated and quietly elegant. Start with the lobby. It's not the showy glass storefront look popularized in the 1960s and 1970s; rather, a hushed, intimate rotunda of marble floors, mahogany-paneled walls and twin elevators sheathed in

ABOVE: *Spectacular views overlooking Central Park and the reservoir are enjoyed from many of the residences at 1049 Fifth Avenue.* TOP RIGHT: *Mahogany-paneled libraries underscore the elegance of the pre-war layouts.* BOTTOM RIGHT: *The interiors are distinguished by pleasing proportions, exquisite details and meticulously executed finishes. Classic Fifth Avenue grandeur defines the living room shown here, a gracious entertaining area embellished with a coffered ceiling, crown moldings and spectacular Central Park view.*

OPPOSITE: *Family living areas include formal dining rooms with an adjacent butler's pantry to facilitate gracious entertaining.* LEFT: *As with all great Fifth Avenue buildings, the focal point is the magnificent lobby, designed as an elegant, intimate space complete with doorman, concierge and elevator operator service.* BELOW: *Eat-in kitchens feature state-of-the-art appliances and technology along with furniture-quality hand-crafted cabinets.*

bronze. Uniformed doormen, elevator operators and a concierge staff are on duty 24 hours a day. On the floors above, hallways are carpeted in a 19th century design custom woven for the building, and damask-covered walls display polished brass sconces.

This return to classical elegance continues within each residence, beginning with the layouts. Jack Heller certainly heeded the words of the late Rosario Candela, the architect for the greatest New York residences ever built, who decreed the city apartment should be comprised of three well-defined areas—for living, for sleeping, and for service. At 1049 Fifth Avenue, raised-panel pocket doors open coffered-ceilinged living rooms into formal dining rooms. Libraries paneled in mahogany are steps away from marble powder rooms. Service entrances provide an alternative access to the state-of-the-art kitchen and pantry areas, and each foyer is positioned to separate these principal rooms from the private accommodations. Through-

out, the floors are of exquisite hand-laid rosewood herringbone-patterned parquet with contrasting borders of ebony.

Walking through a typical residence, there is little sense of living in one of the busiest cities in the world; the quiet is totally unfamiliar to anyone who has lived in Manhattan. Exterior walls consist of three thicknesses of brick, terra cotta and plaster, plus an inner lining of insulation. Similarly, the floors are double-layered concrete topped with a soundproofing cushion beneath the hardwood parquet. The panoramic windows are dual-glazed Chicago-style designs finished outside to complement the masonry facade; inside, to coordinate with the interior decor. Even the most modest apartment in the building has a minimum of two exposures. The full-floor penthouses have four, along with a family room, his-and-her baths and wood-burning fireplaces.

Heller admits he gets more than knee-deep in determining what a home should offer, how it should function, what it

RIGHT: *Rising 23 stories next to the last and loveliest of the Vanderbilt mansions, 1049 Fifth Avenue dates back to 1928. Completely rebuilt throughout, the structure now brilliantly combines pre-war elegance with state-of-the-art technological upgrades, the scope of which have never before been attempted in a New York City residential building.*
OPPOSITE: *In addition to affording a gracious introduction to each residence, foyers act as the transition between living/entertaining spaces and the personal areas of the home.*

🏛 *C*HARACTERISTICS

PROPERTY SIZE: 23-story residential condominium building at 86th Street and Fifth Avenue.

WHEN BUILT/RENOVATED: Pre-war building, originally constructed in 1928 as the Adams Hotel. Completely renovated in the 1990s.

NUMBER OF ROOMS: 45 apartments in total, five to 11 rooms each.

SQUARE FOOTAGE: Ranging from 1,830 to 4,700.

NUMBER OF BEDROOMS: Three or four.

NUMBER OF BATHS: As many as six and one-half.

DISTINCTIVE ARCHITECTURAL DETAILS: Each residence has a mahogany-paneled library, raised panel doors, high-tech gourmet kitchen, marble bathrooms, custom-made cabinets, rosewood herringbone floors with ebony borders, coffered ceilings and crown moldings. The lobby is centered around a magnificent rotunda with marble floor.

SPECIAL APPOINTMENTS AND/OR AMENITIES: State-of-the-art amenities including 12-line telephone systems, room-to-room climate control, ample electrical wiring for computers, faxes, etc. Many living rooms have panoramic Central Park and reservoir views. Penthouse layouts include balconies. Extraordinary soundproofing throughout.

ADDITIONAL HIGHLIGHTS: Deluxe Upper East Side building with white-glove service including doorman and concierge, lobby staff and elevator operators on duty 24 hours a day. Within a short walk of world-renown museums, galleries, restaurants and shops. On the third floor, maid's rooms with baths are available for separate purchase.

should look like. In fact, his rather unorthodox planning procedure often includes creating "families" on index cards with his staff. These people have names and ages and professions. They have sons with hobbies and daughters breaking up with boyfriends and guests that never leave. They commute and they cook—or they have a cook. Explains Heller, "We go through this and we say 'how do they use their homes, what's important to them and what isn't?'...it makes homes that work better for people."

Behind the marble bathroom walls, the mahogany cabinets and the granite counters, above the coffered ceilings and beneath the rosewood floors, the "works" of each apartment are unprecedented in residential construction and will remain high-tech into the next century. There's 12-line telephone cabling, pre-wired C.A.T.V. outlets in every room, abundant electrical power to accommodate the most demanding computer systems and appliances, full laundry facilities, and walk-in closets with automatic illumination. Room-to-room climate controls allow a catering staff to work in a kitchen at 65 degrees while an infant recovering from a cold can sleep in an 80-degree nursery.

To Jack Heller, the creation of 1049 Fifth Avenue was important for many reasons, not the least of which was the attempt to "build the best without compromise." Judging from the finished product, he has indeed succeeded.

Photography by Michael W. Smith.

1049 Fifth Avenue was presented in Unique Homes by Heller Macaulay Equities Incorporated, New York, New York.

Bellavista

Santa Ana, Costa Rica

The setting alone is a beguiling thing of beauty: waves of yellow day lilies pointing the way to gardens of mango trees and lushly spreading ficus encircled in the tropical colors of hibiscus, bougainvillea and impatiens. Fragrance comes from established plantings of gardenia and jasmine, while the Pacific Ocean affords a not-so-distant focal point of endless blue. On five acres in the beautiful Coastal Highlands of Costa Rica, just 15 minutes from San Jose, Bellavista represents four years of planning, cultivating, construction and incomparable design in a country known as "the world's protector of environmental resources." Between the Pacific Ocean and the Caribbean Sea, here is a home that celebrates the riches of its landscape, and rewards its owners in an environment of unmatched artistic achievement.

OPPOSITE: *Ionic columns, heavy wood beams and shining terrazzo flooring define the spacious wraparound veranda, outfitted with antiqued custom rattan furniture, 18th century-style cedar benches and leafy local ferns.* ABOVE: *Grecian lotus leaf pillars adorn the pool house, containing tiled hot and cold Jacuzzis, a sauna, seating area and piped-in music. There is an adjacent gazebo with barbecue and wet bar, while the solar-heated pool itself is done in one-inch blue mosaic tiles.*

BELOW: *In the evening, the view to the west includes the sun setting behind distant mountains and the lights in the valley below.* BOTTOM: *The Spanish Revival-style main house is nestled against a verdant hillside.*

🏛
$\mathcal{C}$HARACTERISTICS

PROPERTY SIZE: Five acres.

ARCHITECTURAL STYLE: Spanish Revival style.

WHEN BUILT/RENOVATED: Built 1988 to 1992.

NUMBER OF ROOMS: 12.

SQUARE FOOTAGE: 14,000 under roof.

NUMBER OF BEDROOMS: Four.

OUTBUILDINGS: Pool house with hot and cold spas, sauna, two baths and trellis-style leaded glass wall. Gazebo with barbecue and wet bar, two-bedroom manager's house with gardener's quarters below, dog kennels, staff house, workshop, plant house, and housing for two 5,000-gallon reservoir tanks.

DISTINCTIVE ARCHITECTURAL DETAILS: Uniquely carved doors, large veranda along two elevations with Ionic columns, shining terrazzo floors, side terrace to sandstone pool deck, French doors, wood parquet floors, flower-filled atrium backed by stained glass wall of floral patterns.

SPECIAL APPOINTMENTS AND/OR AMENITIES: Wonderful vistas throughout of distant mountains and the Pacific Ocean. Owner's office located off main library, beautiful entertaining-size kitchen. Rare Russian tribal tapestry in living room. Servant's area with tool room, bedroom and bath.

ADDITIONAL HIGHLIGHTS: Elliptical swimming pool (55' x 35') done in one-inch mosaic tiles, iron entry gates opening onto lavish gardens, vegetable garden and coffee grove near edge of property, mountain and volcano views. Within 15 minutes of golf, horseback riding, country clubs, international airport and sophisticated shopping, dining and entertainment.

Walls of salmon-colored stucco have an appropriately earthy, sun-dried look, while Ionic columns provide elegant support for the veranda that wraps around two sides of the house. A spacious side terrace reaches out to a large sandstone deck, and beyond to a sculpted pool lined with mosaic tiles of pure indigo. A columned open-air pool house/cabana with hot and cold Jacuzzis and a vine-covered gazebo with barbecue and wet bar are nearby. Fresh air and benevolent sunshine are indigenous to the home; whether indoors or out, openness prevails.

The interior captures a striking balance of warm and cool, where floors of smooth terrazzo and hand-painted tile extend into the mellowness of cultivated wood parquet. The quiet comfort of a library filled with

ABOVE: *Hanging on the wall of the living room is a 200-year-old Russian tribal tapestry. To the right of this are folding doors that open to the dining room.* LEFT: *A superb Costa Rican billiard table is found in the library. Adjoining this room is a flower-filled atrium with wall-sized stained-glass garden scene.*

wood beams and 18th century English armchairs is a window away from the flower-filled atrium, its garden motif mirrored in a floral scene of stained glass. There is a visual bounty in each juxtaposition, from the papyrus-patterned tiles and chestnut-colored cabinets in the Egyptian-style master bath, to the fabulous doorways painstakingly carved with depictions of flora and fauna native to Costa Rica.

In these 14,000 square feet, one sees the owner's preference for all things native, along with a penchant for

collecting of a more eclectic nature. Beneath the heavy wood porch beams are cedar benches in the 18th century style of the Central American Highlands. Beside two Georgian English side chairs in the entrance hall is a majestic antique Chinese vase. The dining room features a Persian carpet, Victorian-style mirror and hand-carved Spanish hutch. And in the living room, above a marble side table, hangs an 18th century Russian tapestry. Common to every room, though, is the finest work of Costa Rican artisans along with every conceivable com-

LEFT: *Hand-carved cabinetry depicting birds and flowers native to Costa Rica adorns the kitchen, also featuring top-of-the-line American appliances and hand-painted floor tiles.* BELOW: *The veranda extends the living/entertaining space to the outdoors.* BOTTOM: *The artistry that has gone into the pool certainly makes it one-of-a-kind.*

fort known to the modern world.

In the kitchen and adjoining breakfast room, where the view is of the veranda and pool, one tends not to focus on the finest in American cooking appliances. In bedrooms filled with hand-carved furnishings, Guatemalan textiles and walls of windows, it's easy to overlook—until bedtime, that is—the luxurious mattresses of goose down. Beyond the flower and vegetable gardens, the fruit trees and coffee grove, few ever see the "works" of the place: the manager's house and gardener's quarters, the dog kennels, plant house and sophisticated reservoir tanks. Yet, as much attention has been paid to the engineering as to the elegance of the place.

In a solar heated swimming pool that measures 55 by 35 feet and reaches depths of up to 14 feet, the entire surface is covered in one-inch mosaic tiles from Madrid. Each has been laid piece by piece—the total number of tiles probably around half a million or so. It is merely one of the many gestures of inimitable artistry—one of the labors of love—at Bellavista.

Photography by Alex Atevich.

Bellavista was presented in Unique Homes by Elizabeth H. Hand, Portfolio Properties, Chicago, Illinois.

Homage to the Modernists

In a sanctuary away from the city that at first appears more corporate park than private residence, the son of a Westchester County real estate developer took charge of building a home for his parents that pays tribute to the masters of modern-age architecture. From the rear, one recognizes the gleaming white games in space popularized by Richard Meier. Through enormous walls of windows, Le Corbusier's vision of "masses in light" is echoed some 70 years after his time. We see the inner logic established by Gropius in Europe, the outward calm of Mies van der Rohe and the magical suspension of Buckminster Fuller.

The home is a technological time machine into the next millennium—a dizzying display of steel and glass set squarely on a mountaintop overlooking the Palisades. But it is still a home, and despite structural order and powerful good looks, it is a haven for both quiet reflection and spontaneous fun.

A former student of finance and economics who took an active interest in his father's business some years back, Ira Shapiro explained, "I saw this as a tremendous opportunity to work with my father. He and my mother scrutinized over every last detail, and then I took the completed blueprints and set out to build the house with John Grosfeld of the award-winning Grosfeld Partnership based in Manhattan. The first challenge was to blast away the top of the mountain so that a shelf could be created for the foundation."

Ira, a seasoned bi-athlete, and his father, a masters division champion in racquetball, created an at-home resort with tennis court, indoor and outdoor pools, fitness rooms, massage areas, whirlpool and steam baths, plus racquetball courts outside and in. Yet, he seems to find his greatest thrill in the mere visual experience the house has to offer. The never-ending wall of marble rising above the living room

OPPOSITE: *From its mountaintop setting, this contemporary mansion surveys a panorama that extends some 40 miles in all directions.* LEFT: *Commanding attention in the living room is the marble fireplace wall, which rises two and one-half stories and is flanked by large windows framing breathtaking views.* BELOW: *The contemporary surroundings of the dining room beautifully set off the Frank Lloyd Wright table and chairs.*

153

RIGHT: *Designed by the award-winning Grosfield Partnership of New York City, the home is a masterpiece of fine architectural design, painstaking craftsmanship and contemporary fashion. At every turn, large window expanses take advantage of the stunning views.*
OPPOSITE TOP: *The 63-foot lap pool is part of a lower-level recreation center that includes an exercise room, massage room, steam room, dressing room with bath, and racquetball court with spectator lounge.*
OPPOSITE BOTTOM: *A second exercise room is featured as part of the third-floor master suite.*

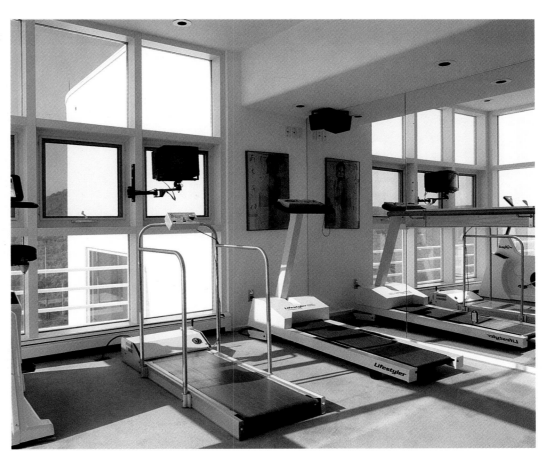

fireplace was selected from a slab by his parents when they searched out a quarry in Italy. He softened the hard-edge geometry with round corners at every turn, and mellowed the floors with white quarter oak stained to a warm amber. Glass curtain walls opened the home to bird's-eye views over the treetops, and a 5,000-square-foot entertainment terrace was cantilevered into the edge of the mountainside.

When asked how one goes about furnishing a home of more than 22 rooms and 21,000 square feet of interior space linked by sweeping galleries, bridges and balconies, Ira Shapiro grows quiet, then succinct. "Very, very slow-ly." He, his three brothers and two sisters each put the finishing touches on their own bedrooms, while the more public spaces became a museum-quality backdrop

CHARACTERISTICS

PROPERTY SIZE: 13 mountaintop acres.

ARCHITECTURAL STYLE: Contemporary.

WHEN BUILT/RENOVATED: Built in 1987.

NUMBER OF ROOMS: 22-plus.

SQUARE FOOTAGE: 21,000.

NUMBER OF BEDROOMS: Seven (not including staff quarters).

NUMBER OF BATHS: Six full, two half-baths.

DISTINCTIVE ARCHITECTURAL DETAILS: 22-foot ceilings, glass curtain walls, sweeping interior bridges, galleries and floating staircases, decks, solid-wood doors, 26-foot-high Italian marble fireplace wall.

SPECIAL APPOINTMENTS AND/OR AMENITIES: Catering-style kitchen plus summer kitchen, billiard and media rooms, indoor 63-foot lap pool, outdoor pool, racquetball and paddle tennis courts, eight-foot television screen in master suite, two exercise/fitness centers, plus high-tech systems for security, climate control, sound and lighting.

ADDITIONAL HIGHLIGHTS: Unmatched surroundings of mountains and woodlands, with views stretching 40 miles to New York City.

for important pieces such as the Frank Lloyd Wright table and chairs in the dining room and, in the living room, a couch featuring a unique accordion-backed design which allows for unlimited seating configurations.

An architectural critic long before he made his mark as an architect, Philip Johnson once wrote, "Merely that a building works is not sufficient. If the business of getting the house to run well takes precedence over your artistic invention, the result won't be architecture at all; merely an assemblage of useful parts." Finding that right balance of form and function is perhaps what the Shapiros have accomplished best. One never seems cognizant of the "works," such as 42 combined zones of heating and air-conditioning, or the state-of-the-art sound, fire, security and lighting systems. What prevails is a calm and clarity without pretense or ponderous embellishment.

So, too, has the right balance been struck between architecture and setting. Contemporary design has found a home in the midst of 13 spectacular acres with 40-mile views all around, and nature has met modernism with a timeless strength of its own.

Photography by Lorna McIntyre Studio.

This mountaintop contemporary was presented in Unique Homes by Naomi Friedman, Friedman Associates, Saddle River, New Jersey.

OPPOSITE: *Encompassing 13 acres carved out of a mountaintop, this private estate is virtually a resort unto itself, yet it is only 40 minutes to the heart of Manhattan.* LEFT: *A heated outdoor pool and Jacuzzi highlight the enormous entertainment terrace.*

157

Urban Aerie

Chicago, Illinois

Chicago's Great Fire of 1871, when a city of wooden structures was leveled to a blank canvas, still ranks right up there with the country's most catastrophic events of all time. Ironically, however, no single event has likely had a more sweeping impact on modern architecture in the Western world. This is the city that virtually invented the skyscraper and metal frame construction, where the Chicago School of Architecture bested Le Corbusier's glass curtain walls, philosopher Louis Sullivan propagated "form follows function" and Frank Lloyd Wright began building his own home at age 22. Verticality became the mode of the day and each successive megastructure instilled a sense of civic prosperity—a "reach for the sky" mentality. Any vestige of Chicago's architectural heritage had been destroyed by that fire; the slate had been wiped clean, so to speak, making it possible for an age of enlightenment in the Second City.

Chicago has been evolving ever since, except perhaps for some of its eastern fringes along Lake Michigan, which will forever remain happily low-rise and residential. A short walk west the horizon heightens dramatically—the world's tallest and third-tallest buildings (the Sears Tower and John

OPPOSITE: *One of the downtown Chicago views enjoyed from The Condominium Residences at Chicago Place.* ABOVE: *Sweeping vistas of the city skyline and Lake Michigan heighten the spaciousness of each layout.*

159

Hancock Center) still measuring sticks for any Chicago developer with big ideas.

The cutting edge skyline that gave the Chicago School impetus for experimentation in commercial design during the post-war years continues to offer inspiration to architects such as Chicago-based Coldwell Solomon Benz, whose newly completed 49-story tower, The Condominium Residences at Chicago Place, is the city's latest landmark of well-moneyed good looks. Like the Four Seasons Hotel which rises above Bloomingdale's, or The Ritz Carlton which was built over Water Tower Place, this white-glove building looms atop an eight-story commercial center. Saks Fifth Avenue, Bockwinkel's European Gourmet Market and another 50 specialty shops on the "foundation" floors make this the Trump Tower of Chicago—though most will maintain the view is even better.

The two principal orientations are east, beyond the rooftops to Lake Michigan (four blocks away); and west, with sunsets and city lights over Chicago's famous Loop,

OPPOSITE TOP: *The elegant appointments and wonderful views that grace the main rooms of each residence can also be found in the master bedroom.* OPPOSITE BOTTOM: *Interesting architectural details and abundant natural light embellish each layout.* ABOVE: *Lustrous wood paneling is only one example of the superior custom finishes that can be included in the interior decoration.*

ABOVE: *Window walls not only make breathtaking views an integral part of the interior design, they create a dramatic backdrop for grand entertaining.* OPPOSITE TOP: *Ceilings eight and one-half feet high and lovely moldings contribute to living spaces that are both gracious and inviting.* OPPOSITE BOTTOM: *A health club with indoor lap pool is only one of the many amenities offered to residents.*

the city's business and financial nerve center. Buildings of equal and even higher stature dwarf the 1869 yellow stone water tower below—the only downtown building which still remained after the Great Fire. Its fake battlements, crenellations and wispy turrets prompted Oscar Wilde to call it a "monstrosity" when he came to town in 1882, though it's a somewhat endearing reminder of where the city came from.

The location of The Condominium Residences at Chicago Place—a few steps from Michigan Avenue's "Miracle Mile"—is of great consolation to those who were born to shop at Tiffany's and Chanel, do lunch at The Palm and live an otherwise unflappable life in the gustiest of towns. The $100 million construction of these condominiums took place in the heaviest of years recession-wise, from 1988 to 1992, but with a 70 percent sell-out by mid-1993, the developers at Brookfield Illinois II, Inc. have reason to be pleased. Upon completion, model apartments were fashioned by award-winning interior designer John Robert Wiltgen who played up the views with lustrous, reflective services while showing sensible restraint when it came to excesses. Window dressings are elegantly spartan. Paneling is mellow and hushed.

Lighting is soft and indirect. It's an adult look for an adult building.

Of the some 200 total apartments, 10 were designed as duplex penthouses with floor-to-ceiling bay windows overlooking Lake Michigan. Layouts of nearly 4,000 square feet provide the added dimensions for enormous walk-in closets, kitchens generously countered in granite, large marble baths and sweeping living and entertaining areas. Interior French doors have a minimal Arts & Crafts look reminiscent of Frank Lloyd Wright's window patterns, while deeply set ceiling moldings recall an even more established style.

Those who make their home at The Condominium Residences at Chicago Place have at their disposal all the amenities of a grande luxe hotel: round-the-clock doormen, indoor valet parking, concierge and mailroom services, hospitality and conference rooms, plus a health club on site with exercise rooms and an indoor lap pool. While the building has not set new heights among the city's great skyscrapers, it has unquestionably set some new and very high standards.

Photography by Steve Hall, © Hedrich-Blessing.

ᛉHARACTERISTICS

ARCHITECTURAL STYLE: Striking 49-story high-rise tower.
DISTINCTIVE ARCHITECTURAL DETAILS: Floor-to-ceiling bay windows capturing city and lake views, marble master baths, granite countertops and lacquer cabinets by Scavolini.
SPECIAL APPOINTMENTS AND/OR AMENITIES: Gourmet kitchens with General Electric Monogram appliances, gigantic walk-in closets, zoned and individually controlled heating and air conditioning. World-class services include 24-hour doormen, electronic surveillance security system, secure indoor valet parking, concierge and mailroom. There is also a hospitality room with kitchen for up to 100 people, a conference room accommodating 25, and a health club featuring exercise rooms and indoor lap pool.
ADDITIONAL HIGHLIGHTS: Direct access to Saks Fifth Avenue, Bockwinkel's European Gourmet Market and over 50 specialty stores and restaurants.

Landmark on the Peninsula

The San Francisco Peninsula has long harbored some of the most exquisite estates in the country. Fortunes were made here in the lucrative days of redwood logging during the 19th century, though it was the "bonanza kings" of mining and transportation who, somewhat later, established the peninsula as a hot spot for country living with a touch of class. Tracing the crests of the Santa Cruz Mountains between San Francisco Bay and the Pacific Ocean, you'll encounter many quaint reminders of earlier times: adobe homesteads from the Spanish and Mexican days, 19th century lighthouses and small communities that began as fishing villages. You'll also encounter some old-money mansions such as Ralston Hall, built by the owner of the San Francisco's Palace Hotel, the Crocker's Uplands (now a private school in Burlingame) and the 700-acre Woodside estate known as Filoli, now deeded to the National Trust for Historic Preservation.

OPPOSITE TOP: *Magnificent gates stand guard at the entrance to Miraflores.* LEFT: *The grand entry hall focuses on a graceful winding staircase and a 24-candle chandelier of solid bronze imported from England.* ABOVE: *The entry drive leads to a cobblestone courtyard with fountain that fronts the home. Built in 1939 in the Monterey Colonial style, the residence has been completely restored to preserve the superior design and artistry exhibited throughout.*

CHARACTERISTICS

PROPERTY SIZE: 21-plus acres on the San Francisco Peninsula.

ARCHITECTURAL STYLE: Monterey Colonial.

WHEN BUILT/RENOVATED: Built in 1939 and thoroughly restored and improved.

SQUARE FOOTAGE: 10,000.

NUMBER OF BEDROOMS: Eight (exclusive of guest house).

NUMBER OF BATHS: 10½.

OUTBUILDINGS: Self-contained one-bedroom guest house, two-car garage, four-car garage, cabana dressing room and bath, seven-stall horse barn with tack and feed rooms, wash rack, paddocks.

DISTINCTIVE ARCHITECTURAL DETAILS: Custom wood and tile floors, bay windows, 19th century bar, 18th century Georgian pine paneling, solid cherry cabinets, imported fixtures. Rosette-carved winding staircase in reception hall. Fireplaces in living room, library, dining room, master bedroom and sitting room.

SPECIAL APPOINTMENTS AND/OR AMENITIES: Main house has attached guest apartment, temperature-controlled wine cellar and tasting room, exercise room/gym, workroom/study, fabulous kitchen with breakfast area and butler's pantry. Decks and terraces overlook pool with koi pond and rock waterfall.

ADDITIONAL HIGHLIGHTS: Pool, tennis court and equestrian facilities. The grounds incorporate approximately 100 mature trees (redwoods, pines and oaks primarily) plus brick and rock pathways winding through gardens of Japanese maples, purple plums, flowering magnolias and beautiful flower beds.

Not far from Filoli's glorious Georgian-style manor (featured on the television series "Dynasty") stands a more private but no less remarkable property, Miraflores. Built in 1939, it is a lovingly restored Monterey Colonial on an irreplaceable 21 acres with unending views in every direction. Over 100 mature trees on the grounds include massive redwoods, towering pines and oaks plus flowering magnolias, purple plums and Japanese maples. Amid gardens fashioned by landscape architect Peter Wright Shaw, meandering brick and rock pathways explore colorful flower beds, a private redwood grove, pool and guest facilities, and a sizable equine complex. At the heart of it all, the home, like a generous host, reaches out in not one but many grand gestures.

Beyond the privately gated entrance, a cobblestone courtyard and fountain introduce the 10,000-square-foot residence, its interiors befitting a fine collection of antiques and important artwork. Among the priceless fittings are early 18th century paneling in the formal dining room, brought from a home in London, and an antique mahogany gentleman's bar which dates back to 1840. In the grand entry hall, where a rosette-carved winding staircase rises to the second floor, there hangs a 24-candle solid bronze chandelier imported from England.

OPPOSITE TOP: *Georgian pine paneling taken from an early 18th century house in London and a beautifully carved wooden mantel lend visual warmth to the formal dining room. A large window bay provides abundant natural light and frames a lovely view of the surrounding grounds.* OPPOSITE BOTTOM: *A spectacular waterfall and koi pond accentuate the sun-drenched pool and spa area.* BELOW: *Large enough to easily accommodate evenings of entertaining, the living room centers around a handsome black marble fireplace. The library and enclosed porch open off of this room.*

ABOVE: *Large, open spaces make the master suite a truly comfortable retreat. It includes panoramic views, a fireplace and his-and-her baths—his paneled in Honduran mahogany, hers with a whirlpool tub and separate shower.* TOP RIGHT: *The paneled library includes a fireplace, built-in bookshelves, file cabinets, video and audio cabinets, and a private staircase that leads up to the master suite.* BOTTOM RIGHT: *The outstanding connoisseur's kitchen features solid cherry wood cabinets and a butcher block island equipped with Jenn-Air deep-fryer and grill.*

This is not, however, a museum. It is a sun-filled home of flowing space and luxurious comfort. The easy airiness of the layout is repeated from one room to the next. An enclosed, screened and windowed porch with wet bar overlooks the owner's cutting garden. The library, complete with audio/video cabinetry, continues its panoramic views up a private staircase to the master suite. Both the dining room and kitchen focus on broad window bays, and a mirrored gym downstairs opens to the pool, spa and tennis court. Entertaining is easy outdoors, intimate in the wine tasting room, and elegant in the candle and fire light of the dining room. Guests who find their way to the kitchen, though, may never want to leave. Cabinets of solid cherry, Traulsen and Montague appliances, butcher-block counters and gleaming copper pots hanging from antique meat hooks create a most inviting mood. The floor, a custom blend of tile and wood, leads on to an adjoining butler's pantry.

Beyond the main residence, a separate guest house augments the accommodations, while closer to the home, the pool provides a wonderful focus of water. The spectacular waterfall and koi pond are integrated into a leafy landscape that gives way to a panorama of distant hills, and the surrounding terraces—like the redwood decks and brick patios—are open to the sunshine. Sharing the pool dressing room and bath is a tennis court complete with backboard and viewing deck. Down the hill from the residential grounds, and accessed by a separate service road, are horse facilities including seven stalls, feed and tack rooms, wash rack, paddocks and a large riding/training ring.

This property is so complete in privacy that it seems virtually impossible that the San Francisco and San Jose International Airports and Silicon Valley are only 30 minutes distant. The frenetic pace of urban life is worlds away; rush hour is non-existent. What does thrive here, however, is the art of living well.

Photography by Leslie Venners.

Miraflores was presented in Unique Homes by Mary S. Gullixson, Fox & Carskadon, Menlo Park, California.

A Grand Scale
PERSPECTIVE

The innovative desert home of celebrated interior designer Steve Chase, built in collaboration with architects Richard Holden and William Carl Johnson, magically integrates itself into its dramatic surroundings at the base of a mountain in prestigious Thunderbird Cove.

the Desert

When it comes to his own house, Steve Chase does not really care about curtains, carpets, rooms with doors, lacquer, chintz or anything else that might detract from pure architectural dialogue. It's a bit of an anomaly, given he's one of the most sought-after interior designers in the country. A denizen of the desert for well over 20 years, Chase has an affinity for both the solidly grounded and the spiritual, an aesthetic clearly defined at his home in Rancho Mirage. Here, his very frank and earthy vision is seen in a rare unity of art, architecture and the outdoors.

His home is an 11,000-square-foot temple which, like all great shrines, offers a reverent backdrop for being at one with the world. Architectural "order" is defined in large interior columns and pillar-like saguaro cacti, in aggregate floors that find their natural extension to the desert ground, and in the indigenous strength of rock, granite and concrete. *Architectural Digest* called it "conceptual power." Steve Chase refers to it as "a house

without compromises." There are associations drawn to some of Chase's mentors, among them Luis Barragan, Gaudi and Frank Lloyd Wright, though the owner/designer maintains, "I have always attempted to reinterpret the ideas within my own vocabulary of form."

The house sits at the foot of the Santa Rosa Mountains, in an austere landscape of rugged boulders, big sky and timeless mystery that seems endemic to the California desert. It was here that Steve Chase set out to create a oneness of indoors and out, planning a home where every room found a natural integration with the gardens. A forest of saguaro grows just beyond the living room windows. The glass wall off the master suite overlooks a fish pond tucked within a grove of ocotillo. From yet another elevation, orderly groupings of golden barrel cactus look up to palo verde and mesquite trees. The centerpiece of Chase's four desert gardens is the pool terrace, a visual treat that includes a waterfall splashing into a Jacuzzi and four unique concrete chaises longues.

Over the years the designer has established a collection of contemporary art that has a venerable home here thanks to the minimalist surfaces of stone, stucco, glass and other natural materials. On an onyx table stands a sculpture by Michael Todd. In the dining room, beneath a wall-size Japanese screen by Shirvu Morita, is a wooden bowl by Ed Moulthrop. A Helen Frankenthaler painting has a prominent position over the living room sofa. The collection also includes works by Frank Stella, Kenneth Noland and Jules Olitski. Remarked the designer in *Palm Springs Life*, "Furniture doesn't mean a lot to me. The art does, the garden does."

Unlike many of his contemporaries in the design world, Steve Chase has always been drawn to the initial act of architecture, not just the trappings that follow. By the age of three he was constructing cities out of wooden blocks—an urge that matured steadily through his years at Rhode Island School of Design and the Art Center School in Los Angeles. By 1967 he was working with the

OPPOSITE: *In one of the home's six bedrooms, the owner's passion for collecting art is evident. The glass block wall, aggregate stone flooring and high ceiling all accentuate the inviting ambience of the space.* ABOVE: *The pool area—complete with a waterfall that cascades into a spa and a pool pavilion with outdoor kitchen—is the centerpiece of the magnificent grounds. Four formed-in-place concrete chaises longues set atop tile bases occupy a prominent place just above the waters of the pool.*

The living room is characteristic of the open, airy spaces that define the approximately 11,000-square-foot layout. The design affords areas that are intimate yet never confining. The result is a unique environment where two or two hundred people can be entertained with ease.

🏛

CHARACTERISTICS

PROPERTY SIZE: One and three-quarter desert acres at the base of a mountain.

ARCHITECTURAL STYLE: Desert contemporary.

SQUARE FOOTAGE: Approximately 11,000.

NUMBER OF BEDROOMS: Six.

NUMBER OF BATHS: Eight.

OUTBUILDINGS: Pool-side guest house, pool pavilion with outdoor kitchen, three-car garage.

DISTINCTIVE ARCHITECTURAL DETAILS: Textural surfaces including stucco walls, aggregate floors, granite and redwood strip ceilings. Architectural order established through the utilization of large columns, slabs of stone and glass block walls.

SPECIAL APPOINTMENTS AND/OR AMENITIES: Four individual gardens designed as natural extensions of the interior. Tennis court, media room, sauna, swimming pool with built-in cast chaises longues. Dramatic landscape lighting.

ADDITIONAL HIGHLIGHTS: This is the Rancho Mirage home of interior designer Steve Chase, located in exclusive Thunderbird Cove. It has been featured in *Architectural Digest* and *Palm Springs Life*.

---

celebrated designer Arthur Elrod; and in 1980, he went out on his own and established Steve Chase Associates. Today in Rancho Mirage, the designer is creating a "neighborhood" that happily shies away from all traditional connotations of the term. He prefers berms over fences, no square plots and no cookie-cutter houses. There isn't any of the "this is my yard, that's your yard" consciousness, he claims, reminding us this is the desert, not Beverly Hills or Dallas.

In the house where he modestly says he's "just the caretaker," Steve Chase has created an oasis of geologic wonder that appears as timeless as the landscape itself. There's an organic sense of belonging along with an extraordinary level of sophistication and comfort. His habitat is his happiness. It seems especially fitting that in this designer's house, the prevailing decor is nature itself.

Photography by Jim Bartsch.

This desert masterpiece was presented in Unique Homes by Susan Canavan and Deirdre Coit, Canavan Coit Inc., Palm Desert, California.

A Contemporary Classic

Old Westbury, Long Island, New York

David Yarom is an admitted dreamer. He came here over 20 years ago from Israel with German-born wife Eva, a young daughter and visions of making a place for himself in America. His first goal was to get his masters degree in systems engineering. Now his first child is getting her masters and thinking seriously about following in her father's footsteps. In 1984, the Yaroms began building the home of their collective dreams on a lushly treed four acres in Old Westbury, an exclusive Long Island village known for its magnificent estate properties. Suffice it to say they didn't exactly hurry this project along; it was three years, some $4,000,000 and countless design experts in the making. When the 15,000-square-foot residence was completed, however, it was clear that it would certainly satisfy the Yaroms' unique ideal of a home that looked as well as it lived.

OPPOSITE: *In setting out to create a contemporary home that is both elegant and relaxing, the Yaroms opted for a layout of open, flowing spaces characterized by visually interesting angled and curved surfaces, custom appointments and outstanding woodwork. Shown here is the view from the living room to the front door and the dining room.* ABOVE: *The influence of Frank Lloyd Wright's work is evident when viewing the facade of the home, which is set low well into the land.*

PROPERTY SIZE: Four acres.

ARCHITECTURAL STYLE: Stone and glass contemporary in ground-hugging style of Frank Lloyd Wright.

WHEN BUILT/RENOVATED: Built in 1988.

NUMBER OF ROOMS: 20.

SQUARE FOOTAGE: 15,000.

NUMBER OF BEDROOMS: Six.

NUMBER OF BATHS: Nine and one-half.

DISTINCTIVE ARCHITECTURAL DETAILS: Built-in pear wood cabinets, custom marble-topped bar in living room, tile flooring imported from Germany, massive stone fireplace in living room, indoor garden, "waterfall" chandelier of Maurano glass in dining room, natural finishes of granite, wood and stone.

SPECIAL APPOINTMENTS AND/OR AMENITIES: Resort setting with 66-foot swimming pool, tennis court, indoor pool with Jacuzzi, plus squash, basketball and volleyball courts. Grounds extensively planted with specimen trees and flowering shrubs to complement the rocky contours of the home.

ADDITIONAL HIGHLIGHTS: Designed and owned by the principals of Nova Studio Ltd., a Long Island-based design firm bringing the best of Italian workmanship, furniture and fittings to contemporary American architecture. Located in Old Westbury, one of Long Island's most sought-after communities.

Today Mr. and Mrs. Yarom are founding partners of Nova Studio Ltd., a company which unites the finest in Italian design and workmanship with a talented firm of American architects headquartered in their own studio. The now four-year-old business was an outgrowth of their own house-building experience, a project which David recalls had one prevailing challenge: "Visualization." In Milan, the Yaroms discovered the work of Dr. Dario Caimi and Franco Asnaghi, interior designers and furniture makers who created many of the fittings for their home and would eventually come to play a significant role in the Nova aesthetic.

The house itself is deceiving from the outside, with its well-anchored, ground-hugging design of stone and glass that appears—in the manner of Frank Lloyd Wright—as if growing from the contours of the land. From this van-

OPPOSITE TOP: *A "waterfall" chandelier comprised of 400 individual links of Maurano glass illuminates a marble and cherry table and Cassina barrel chairs designed by Frank Lloyd Wright in the dining room.* LEFT: *The indoor pool.* TOP: *The informal entertainment area comes complete with bar and kitchenette.* ABOVE: *Lacquer cabinetry, cedar ceiling, granite counters and up-to-date lighting are among the kitchen highlights.*

tage point, one has little sense of the entire lower level, for instance, or of the expanse taken up by the indoor pool, the indoor bamboo garden, and the grand layout of six bedrooms and nine and one-half baths. "We really don't go in for glitz," explains David, adding that their favorite part of the home is the kitchen and its adjoining sitting area overlooking the pool.

The serenity of the home is best seen in an architectural simplicity achieved from natural elements: the "staircase wall" of cabinets in pear wood, the massive stone accent wall in the kitchen, the wraparound facades of glass in the den. "We avoided an overabundance of big mirrors, lacquer and chrome," says the owner, whose preference leans more toward the stylistic purity of barrel

chairs designed by Frank Lloyd Wright, cedar ceilings and a substantial sweep of granite.

The indoor pool is accompanied by another larger one outside, along with an at-home resort which includes an interior squash/racquetball/volleyball court and an all-weather ping-pong table outdoors. An elaborate exercise room, which David says isn't used as often as it should be, is convenient to both pools as well as an informal entertainment area with bar and kitchenette. In his next house, the owner plans to put the workout room closer to the master suite. "A bit more incentive to exercise," he hopes.

The Yaroms maintain their next home will also be closer to the waters of the North Shore. They had younger children in mind when planning the home that,

they admit, "is one big statement." Now they envision a place of several smaller structures and "a bigger garage...at least six cars!" jokes David. They will continue to divide their time between a home on Long Island, the Nova Studio and a ski house nestled near the lifts at Stratton, Vermont.

Would they do it all over again? "Yes," answers David Yarom. Any regrets? "I have a lot of dreams and not enough time to fulfill them all."

Photography by Jon Ortner.
Photo of front facade by Jeff Heatley.

This contemporary classic was presented in Unique Homes by Sandy Binder, Sandy Binder's House of Homes, Mineola, New York.

TOP: *The home's long list of custom features includes these built-in drawers and cabinets located in one of the master suite's two dressing areas.*
ABOVE: *The home's outdoor pool was beautifully designed to be a visual complement to the striking facade. It measures 66 feet in length and provides a wonderful setting for informal summertime entertaining. The four acres of grounds also include a tennis court as well as colorful plantings and a variety of specimen trees.*

Tous Les Siécles

Rancho Santa Fe, California

From the very first approach, where entry gates brought from the Hennessy Cognac Winery in France rise above gardens of blue hibiscus, there is a romantic timelessness to the place. It was built over a period of 19 months less than a decade ago, but its details span countless generations of European artistry, from a willow-edged pond that's a scene straight from Giverny to the 16th and 17th century ironwork framing the balconies and windows. Creating a French country manor seemed a logical choice for the owners, whose buying trips to Europe have long been an annual event; and Rancho Santa Fe allowed the perfect opportunity to make it happen. Back in the early 1980s, they were all set to go with permits and plans for a home in Newport Beach. Then they saw Rancho Santa Fe and said to their architect and long-time friend, Robert Earl, "Make it long!"

And spread out they did, on four acres of grounds and

OPPOSITE: *Gates which once were used at the Hennessy Cognac Winery in France now adorn the entrance to this elaborate estate.* ABOVE: *Viewed from the pool area, the estate residence and its surrounding landscape are both dramatic and inviting. Built in 1985, the home encompasses almost 13,000 square feet of space and offers a wealth of distinctive features brought from Europe.*

gardens with orange groves, a pool, stocked pond, tennis court, large cabana and a 14-bay garage that has been home to their collection of antique and classic cars. It is within the main house, though, that these passionate collectors have created their own time in history. The paintings include pieces from the Barbizon School as well as 19th century landscapes and portraits. Parquet de Versailles floors are featured in the public rooms, along with 18th and 19th century stone fireplaces and trompe l'oeil murals. The bar and tap room is fitted in distressed walnut; the library displays warm Honduran mahogany.

Virtually every fitting in this house of nearly 13,000 square feet has its own story to tell, such as the hundreds of hand-painted tiles from Holland. The owners remember with great fondness their trip to Delft in search of just the right source. In a small mom-and-pop shop with one elf-sized helper, they placed their order for the tiles that would eventually fill the kitchen and pantry areas. When the humble proprietors learned of the quantity

OPPOSITE: *A 19th century French limestone fireplace mantel and Honduran mahogany paneling characterize the elegant library.* TOP: *Ceilings of 20 feet and a floor of Italian Carrara and Verde marble create a magnificent first impression in the grand entry.* ABOVE: *An 18th century fireplace mantel surrounded by trompe l'oeil paneling and 20-foot ceilings are in the family room.*

ABOVE: *The large veran-da affords a spectacular view over rolling lawns to the pool, spa and cabana area.* OPPOSITE TOP: *The lush grounds include a stocked pond surrounded by majestic willows and other speci-men plantings.* OPPOSITE BOTTOM: *Housing for up to 14 cars is provided by the twin buildings that flank the motor court.*

required, they sat in stunned disbelief and finally exclaimed, "That's not possible! Are you building a house like the one on 'Dallas'?" But the tiles did arrive. As did tons of marble selected from a friend's quarry in Carrara. The 17th century Hennessy gates came too, along with the weighty surprise of the massive pilasters that once supported them. "We didn't know we were buying the pilasters as well," explain the owners, who tell how no mathematical genius was ever able to recon-struct the various pieces. They did, however, retain the original capitals.

While their home may well be the size of the Ewing mansion at Southfork Ranch, the similarity stops there. This is a family place where the children fish in the bass-stocked pond and have 10 friends over for lunch by the pool. Neighbors get together and walk into town for din-ner at Milles Fleurs, and Christmas is celebrated with dinner for 50 in the grand foyer, complete with caroling and some old Cole Porter songs around the grand piano. One family member claims that if the walls could talk, they'd say this is a happy place to grow up.

In keeping with this authentic recreation of the European countryside, the grounds offer a lush balance

to the sprawling architectural presence of the home, with its classical columns, double-height Palladian win-dows and ceilings as tall as 20 feet. Courtyards, terraces and walkways are all framed in palms and flower beds. Beside the pond, there's more of a leafy meadow look with interspersed areas of sun and shade. At dusk, the property changes its mood again as landscape lighting focuses on many of the well-tended plantings, and the pool and spa waters display dramatic reflections. Beveled windows, balconies, a sweeping veranda and slate-floored solarium all serve to bring the house closer to its park-like surroundings.

"We love the creative part of building," say the own-ers, which may, to some extent, explain why they have moved to new homes no less than 14 times in their 26-year marriage. But in the house that they've remained in since 1986, living well has been their best love of all.

Photography by Jennifer Harcq.

This magnificent European-inspired estate was presented in Unique Homes by Coldwell Banker/Previews® in Rancho Santa Fe, California.

𝒞 H A R A C T E R I S T I C S

PROPERTY SIZE: Approximately four acres within the Rancho Santa Fe Covenant area.

ARCHITECTURAL STYLE: French country manor.

WHEN BUILT/RENOVATED: Built in 1986.

SQUARE FOOTAGE: 12,750.

NUMBER OF BEDROOMS: Five.

NUMBER OF BATHS: Eight.

DISTINCTIVE ARCHITECTURAL DETAILS: Chinese slate floors, Parquet de Versailles floors, antique French fireplaces, 20-foot ceilings, trompe l'oeil paneling, balconies, leaded windows and finishes of slate, marble, crystal, bronze, walnut and mahogany.

SPECIAL APPOINTMENTS AND/OR AMENITIES: Bar and tap room, flower-arranging room, kitchen with four ovens, master suite with bar and fireplace, 17th century entrance gates from Hennessy Cognac Winery in France, imported hand-painted Delft tiles.

ADDITIONAL HIGHLIGHTS: Stocked pond, orange groves, pool, spa, lighted tennis court, entertainment cabana with kitchen, garage space for 14 cars.

Dean Gardens

Near Atlanta, Georgia

Twenty-two years ago Larry and Lynda Dean, a young Georgia couple of modest means, with three sons under the age of five, started a company on a $500 loan from their two-year-old. "I would have borrowed the money from my oldest boy but we had put his 'legacy' in a mutual fund, and at the time, it was only worth about $350," recalls Larry Dean of the early years. Over a period of two decades his little company, Stockholder Systems, Inc., grew to become a 350-employee computer software empire 25 miles upriver from Atlanta in Norcross, Georgia; and their lives shifted focus on a 60-acre spread known as Dean Gardens.

From March 1988 until September 1992, Larry and Lynda, in tandem with architect Bill Harrison, a few hundred construction workers, assorted laborers and plasterers created what is thought to be the largest private home in Georgia. Where there was once raw Fulton County pastureland along the Chattahoochee, the Deans have fashioned Oriental gardens with a teahouse, waterfalls and bridges crossing a lagoon filled with Japanese koi. They have carved out of the land an 18-hole, par 72 golf course and a man-made lake complete with its own wedding chapel.

The formal gardens were inspired by the Bouchart Gardens near Victoria, British Columbia, and, closer to

TOP LEFT: *The entry drive encircles a fountain in front of the striking mansion at Dean Gardens.* BOTTOM LEFT: *An aerial view of the property gives a true indication of the estate's breathtaking scope.* ABOVE: *Inspired by the Brunelini Cathedral in Florence, Italy, the three and one-half-story rotunda—with its spectacular skylighted dome—is a fitting introduction to the imaginative grand-scale design on view throughout.*

⌂ CHARACTERISTICS

PROPERTY SIZE: 60 acres.

ARCHITECTURAL STYLE: Neo-classical villa.

WHEN BUILT/RENOVATED: Built 1988-1992.

SQUARE FOOTAGE: Approximately 32,000 square feet.

NUMBER OF BEDROOMS: Eight.

NUMBER OF BATHS: 10 full, three half-baths, plus men's and ladies' cabanas

OUTBUILDINGS: 10,000-square-foot carriage house with two two-bedroom apartments, conservatory, amphitheatre, greenskeeper's cottage, wedding chapel plus assorted other dependencies.

DISTINCTIVE ARCHITECTURAL DETAILS: 13 fireplaces, 1950s-style game room, domed rotunda entry, floating spiral staircase to all three floors, French Empire-style grand salon, stained glass windows, balustrades and balconies. Extraordinary custom fittings of rosewood, marble, granite, limestone, crystal and glass.

SPECIAL APPOINTMENTS AND/OR AMENITIES: 3,000-square-foot master suite, indoor ponds and aquariums, caterer's kitchen, Moroccan-style media room, audio and video built-ins. Some 25 water features on property including a fountain imported from Turin, Italy, with added reflecting ponds.

ADDITIONAL HIGHLIGHTS: 18-hole golf course, frontage on the Chattahoochee River, a man-made lake, French, Italian and Oriental gardens, shell-shaped swimming pool, in-house fitness center, grass tennis court and croquet lawn.

home, the Bellingrath Gardens in Mobile, Alabama. They begin to the south and east of the mansion, with a rose garden and wisteria trellises near the amphitheatre and conservatory. There are dramatic French gardens, an estimated half a million tulips and daffodils blooming each spring, and another 200,000 or so plants on the property. Nothing here is half-hearted.

If a view of the Neptune Fountain imported from Turin (one of 25 water features on the property) seems out of place beside Japanese maples shipped in from Oregon and a wedding chapel patterned after one at the Westin Hotel on the island of Kauai, you have missed the point of this fascinating estate. From the onset, Dean Gardens was destined to awe and amaze.

Inside the 32,000-square-foot neo-classical mansion, all is equally eclectic, beginning in a domed rotunda inspired by the Brunelini Cathedral in Florence and culminating in son Christopher's Egyptian bedroom suite and its tomb-like bath complete with hieroglyphics, papyrus leaves, ankhs and a floor of Solenhauffen stone.

OPPOSITE TOP: *Antique Bulgarian chandeliers suspended from a trompe l'oeil ceiling, heavily carved moldings and even built-in aquariums can be found in the baronial dining room.* OPPOSITE BOTTOM: *The octagonal Peacock Room—complete with cappuccino bar—is conducive to relaxed evenings of entertaining.* BELOW: *The grand salon is a majestic two-story room designed as a memorable backdrop for the most lavish of gatherings. This enormous space is flanked on one side by the rotunda, and on the other by a wall of glass that looks out over the fantastic pool area.*

It was Christopher Dean who, at age 21, was given the task of designing the interiors of the home. "We fought endlessly the first year, " laughs his father, "until I figured out that he was right."

"I think there's something special in this house that can please everybody," suggests Christopher Dean. "Most people, when they walk in...they are usually very quiet and their smile just widens with each room they go into." The young designer transformed one parlor into a 1950s game room with soda fountain and ice cream bar, another into a Moroccan-style media center reminiscent of the much-admired decor of Atlanta's historic Fox Theatre. Formal spaces range from the octagonal Peacock Room with its two-ton limestone table set beneath a 43-foot ceiling, to a dining room embellished with antique chandeliers from Bulgaria, oil paintings on

ABOVE: *Elegant guest accommodations are afforded by the Silver Suite.* TOP RIGHT: *The rear of the house opens to a lavish area complete with stunning shell-shaped pool, grand staircases and balconies, garden spots and views overlooking the world-class grounds.* BOTTOM RIGHT: *The Moroccan-style theme that pervades much of the terrace level of the home is reminiscent of the interiors at Atlanta's famous Fox Theatre.*

the cove ceiling and a black lacquer banquet table inlaid with malachite.

One gets the impression that nothing ordinary ever happens here, but the Deans will tell you otherwise. Larry, remembering the day they first moved in, said there was much joy and thanksgiving when the big day finally came, but will never forget the vast clouds of styrofoam nuggets that spilled out of packing boxes and created a sea of white popcorn on the property. "I really passed out over that, and later mentioned to my estate manager that the only thing worse would be to not have hot water for my first shower the next morning."

Indeed, it was a cold shower for Larry Dean the following day; but what a great place to get goose bumps!

Photography by Chuck Rogers.
Photograph on page 191 by Mary Ann Ramsey Smith.

Dean Gardens was presented in Unique Homes by Jason Dean, Coldwell Banker/Previews®, Atlanta, Georgia.

Camelback Villa

Paradise Valley, Arizona

Inspired by the villas of the French Mediterranean, builder Ken Brown has crafted a one-of-a-kind mansion in the middle of the Arizona desert.

BELOW: *The pool area—complete with diving rocks, spa, covered patio and built-in barbecue—fits right in to its natural surroundings.* BOTTOM: *In the enormous entry foyer, the cast stone staircase leading up to the master suite is flanked by a series of windows that step up as well.* TOP RIGHT: *The large stone fireplace is a focal point in the sunken living room.* BOTTOM RIGHT: *The gallery—lined with large glass French doors—provides a sunny approach to both the living room and the dining room.*

It's a mountain and desert landscape of larger-than-life beauty where classical architecture and the untamed West have teamed up in the posh environs of Paradise Valley. The aqua pools set against native boulders and the arid northern slopes of Camelback Mountain are not a mirage, and while arched loggias suggest Old World Tuscany or the sunbaked Riviera, this is indeed the desert of central Arizona. Together, the home and the land display a timeless permanence, along with a gifted new view of what the good life is all about.

In a rambling 10,000-square-foot design of interconnecting colonnades and archways, the home spreads out on only a small portion of its 11 acres. Architect Ken Brown has tempered the landscape in a design that is both formal and welcoming, and always integrated to its surrounds. Standing in the huge entry, this prevailing openness is established at once. While the commanding staircase with balustrade of cast stone has a medieval weightiness, its austerity is softened in a rise of magnificent beveled glass windows that mirror its gradual, curving ascent. In this same space, a beveled glass window wall overlooks the patio, pond and pool, and a door of leaded glass leads on to the gardens.

Built for one of Arizona's oldest and most established families, people with a penchant for French country style, the 14-room interior was largely influenced by ideas collected from their travels abroad. Hand-painted French tiles are coordinated from room to room, as well as outdoors in the diving pool and spa. The family room with its large built-in entertainment unit was styled around a French fireplace dating back three centuries. The centerpiece of the living room is yet another grand-

ABOVE: *A 300-year-old French tile fireplace brings an old world flair to the family room.* OPPOSITE TOP: *A large breakfast room with soaring ceiling and arched windows adjoins the gourmet island kitchen.* OPPOSITE BOTTOM: *Throughout the home, an abundance of glass floods the layout with natural light and maximizes enjoyment of the wonderful views.*

scale fireplace, this one of stone. The domed dining room has exquisitely milled cherry wood floors and a recessed arch for buffet service. Each space has a decidedly European grace, yet each also remains wedded to the Southwest.

The oversized custom French doors seen throughout add limitless dimension to interiors created by Hasbrook Interiors and Antiques, as do charming window seats, wide archways and endless openings to the outdoors. Windows in the beamed living room focus on mountains and city lights. The breakfast room is positioned for effortless access to the covered and open patios facing the pool. In the master suite, one can gaze upon Mummy Mountain from the study, overlook the pool from the bedroom balcony, or take in Camelback Mountain from the sitting room. From one of two master baths, there continues an unending view of the entire east valley.

From one space to the next, there is a remarkable display of hand-crafted artistry. The curving staircases are of cast stone and Saltillo tile. Much of the woodwork and doors are of Honduran mahogany. There are beamed and skylighted ceilings accented with rough-sawn light wood, floors inlaid with cherry wood and tile, plus cupolas, walk-in closets and built in cabinetry.

No less attention has been paid to the engineering of

this remarkable property. There are elevators in each end of the house, mechanical facilities discreetly housed within the six-car garage space, separate laundry and kitchen facilities for the main house and guest residence, and commercial-capacity air conditioning throughout.

For all its extravagances, though, nowhere does the home come together better than at poolside, where architecture and setting reign as one. A covered loggia runs the entire length of the rear facade, its expanse of Saltillo tiles briefly interrupted by a small pond. Beyond, the heated swimming pool and spa are built into a grotto with high diving rocks surrounded by smooth flagstone, sun-drenched lounge areas and breezy palms.

From a position high on the desert mountainside, each elevation of the home fits snugly into the landscape. The horizon is filled with powerful views: Mummy Mountain, the night lights of Scottsdale, Pinnacle Peak and the majestic McDowell range. The inner beauty of the home is surpassed only by its outlook.

Photography by Theodore Wyshyvanuk.

This Camelback villa was presented in Unique Homes by Ellie Shapiro, Coldwell Banker Success Realty, Phoenix, Arizona.

🏛 CHARACTERISTICS

PROPERTY SIZE: 11 acres on Camelback Mountain.

ARCHITECTURAL STYLE: Desert villa with French country elements.

NUMBER OF ROOMS: 14 (in main house).

SQUARE FOOTAGE: Nearly 10,000 (exclusive of covered outdoor areas, garage and guest house facilities).

DISTINCTIVE ARCHITECTURAL DETAILS: Rough-sawn ceilings and decking, tinted windows, hand-crafted millwork of Honduran Mahogany, floors of Saltillo tile and distressed cherry wood, curving staircases of stone and tile, imported hand-painted tiles from France, arching windows and doorways.

SPECIAL APPOINTMENTS AND/OR AMENITIES: Two elevators—one at each end of home. Commercial air conditioning system, open and covered French-tile patios, diving pool with spa and barbecue terrace, exquisite imported fireplaces, built-in window seats, bookcases, vanities and walk-in closets. Interior design by Hasbrook Interiors and Antiques, Inc.

ADDITIONAL HIGHLIGHTS: Self-contained guest house with living room, bedroom, two full baths, kitchen and laundry facilities. Six-car garage. Magical gardens surround this estate with a panorama of Mummy Mountain, the night lights of Scottsdale and Pinnacle Peak, and the majestic McDowell Mountains in the distance. In a quiet Paradise Valley location convenient to fine shopping, dining and golf courses in Scottsdale.

If You Love Fine Homes, You're In Good Company.

Your home is more than just a place to live. It's a symbol of your style, a testament to your individuality. No one understands this more than The Prudential Florida Realty. We share your penchant for fine homes. You might say it's our passion.

That's important. To locate the perfect home requires someone who specializes in prestigious residences, someone whose passion is combined with knowledge,

At The Prudential Florida Realty we are successful because we understand you demand a home as unique as you are.

Orlando? Or a classic Bermuda on Naples Beach? We want to find the home that dazzles you and fills you with delight. The home that feels just right when you walk in the front door.

Choosing the right brokerage is crucial to finding the right home. But please don't consider The Prudential Florida Realty because we have the largest relocation and referral network, more offices, more associates,

skill and a flair for getting the job done in exceptional fashion.

Whether you're from across town, out of state or from a foreign land you want a home that reflects your lifestyle. What will it be? A palace in Palm Beach? A mansion in Miami? A townhouse in Tampa? An exquisite Mizner in Boca Raton? A condo in

more listings, and more sales than any other independent real estate services company in Florida.

Indeed, choose The Prudential Florida Realty because it's comforting to know you're in good company . . . with someone who shares your love for fine homes. We understand Florida, its people, its property and its passions. We are Florida.

The**Prudential**

Florida Realty

For a complimentary copy of our Fine Homes Collection magazine, please call
1-800-BUY-FLA-1

We Are Florida℠

The**Prudential** and ⓖ are registered service marks
of The Prudential Insurance Company of America.
Equal Housing Opportunity. ⌂
An Independently Owned and Operated Member
of The Prudential Real Estate Affiliates, Inc.®

The Pleasure of Your Company
is Requested

You are cordially invited to join us for a
full year (six issues) of UNIQUE HOMES -
your entrée to the finest in available
residential and investment properties.
Your annual subscription will cost
just $24.97–a full 40% off
the newsstand price of $6.95 per issue.

Call Toll-free 1-800-827-0660